Mommyhood Diaries

Living the Chaos One Day at a Time

101 "Day in the Life"
Diaries from Moms
Around the World

Julie Watson Smith

Wyatt-MacKenzie Publishing, Inc.
DEADWOOD, OREGON

To my always supportive husband, John:
Without you, I would never be me.

To my three, silly muses, Finnegan, Ainsley and Bailey Blu:
Thank you for bringing the chaos to my life.

To my angel on Earth, Roselia:
You are, by far, the most sincere person I've ever met.

To my parents:
How did you get through the day with me as your child?

And, finally, to moms worldwide:
Mary McCarthy once said that we are the hero
of our own story. You are also the hero of your child's story.
I wish you the best life has to offer.

Mommyhood Diaries: Living the Chaos One Day at a Time

by Julie Watson Smith

ISBN: 1-932279-16-4

Library of Congress Control Number: 2005933289

www.wymacpublishing.com

Published by The Mom-Writers Publishing Cooperative
Wyatt-MacKenzie Publishing, Inc., Deadwood, OR
www.WyMacPublishing.com (541) 964-3314

Requests for permission or further information should be addressed to: Wyatt-MacKenzie Publishing, 15115 Highway 36, Deadwood, Oregon 97430

Printed in the United States of America

Table of Contents:
What's in a Day

You can steer yourself in any direction you choose.

~Dr. Seuss

* *Name changed to protect identity*

Foreword

by Jessica Denay

When you've found your center, overcome your obstacles, empower other moms to do the same.

~ Hot Moms Club Mantra

Mommyhood Diaries is a collection of touching journals to help moms take comfort in the fact that they are not alone—in fact, it's just the opposite! There has always been something about motherhood that connects us all, a connection that defies race, class, or age. Motherhood is indeed the great equalizer! It's true that we all have that never-ending, always-growing to-do list, break-up arguments, tantrums and spills and messes.

Yes, we all have moments of sheer madness. It comes with the title "MOM." However, as moms we manage to juggle carpools, soccer games, work, and PTA meetings—often with a toddler strapped to our hip—we are nothing short of "Hot Mom Superheroes" Surely, we can find five minutes to indulge ourselves and our spirit daily. Motherhood can indeed be chaotic, but it is so important not to lose yourself in the process. I encourage you to make it an absolute priority to put yourself on your to-do list.

Now, as all of the amazing moms in this book, I have journaled my entire day. I have chosen to leave out all the errands, the frustrating moments, the phone calls. After that, I am left with only what is truly important.

7:00 AM My five-year-old son crawls into bed with me. We snuggle, wrestle… I relish this time; he lets me kiss him without protest.

10:15 AM My son came up and hugged me for no reason.

1:00 PM Talked to my mom - I told her that I said something to my son this week that she always said to me. She laughed.

4:45 PM Put down the phone and step away from the computer for 15 minutes. I sit outside in the sun by myself to catch my breath, relax.

4:53 PM Okay, so it was only eight minutes. But it was relaxing, and it was mine!

6:30 PM Dinner with my son and my boyfriend. Decided to make it a picnic dinner tonight. Just set up a blanket in the living room, and we ate there. It is amazing how just moving the meal can add a little excitement and adventure.

8:00 PM Story time! I love his facial expressions and how excited he gets about his books; he is the most beautiful child in the world!

8:30 PM Bedtime! Oooh - how I wish it was my bedtime, but back to work.

No matter what chaos your day holds, remember to capture those magical moments with your children, and remember to nurture your spirit—guilt free! Finding my center and maintaining my balance has no doubt made me a better and more effective mom And, as this book so wonderfully illustrates, motherhood can be overwhelming, but YOU ARE NOT ALONE! Stay inspired, because you have certainly inspired me. There have been many days when I wonder how I can possibly keep doing it all; this book is a gentle reminder of why I became a mom, followed my dreams and started the Hot Moms Club. I wanted to inspire and empower moms everywhere.

Rock on, Hot Moms!

~ Jessica Denay
"There's no stopping me now" mother of one
HotMomsClub HMCmagazine.com

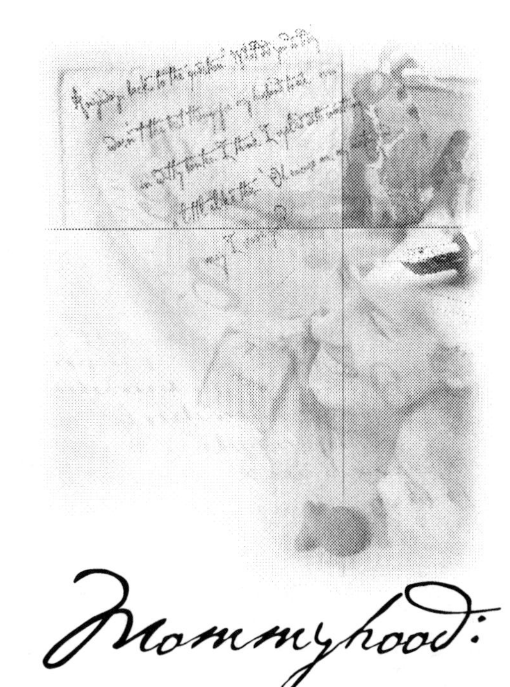

Mommyhood:

Learning, Living, and Loving the Chaos

Apparently, there is nothing that cannot happen today.

~ Mark Twain

Have you ever had one of "those days"? I have—more often than I'd like to admit. However, there was one day, in particular, that stands out. It was a day that left me frazzled and frustrated. It was the day Mommyhood was conceived.

The day started out simply enough. I woke up, fed the kids, and was just about to hop in the shower when I heard "it." CRASH! BANG! BOOM! It was followed by a meek "Uh-oh." Wrapped in a towel, I rushed into the living room to one small boy standing near an island of broken glass amidst of sea of blue-stained white carpet. My son had broken my husband's collection of specialty bottles. Unfortunately, the bottles were filled with beer—very blue beer, to be exact. Now, before you start questioning my childproofing methods, the bottles had been stored on a high shelf. I, however, had underestimated the power of a determined toddler. And, as Murphy's Law would have it, we were putting our house on the market to sell the next day.

Several bottles of bleach, a can of air freshener and a tub of carpet cleaner later, I felt that I had overcome adversity and smiled in the face of defeat. Okay, okay. I really just turned the deep blue stain to a slightly azul-tinged white mass, but I'll take kudos where I can. Unfortunately, my feelings of elation were soon squashed with constant battles, tantrums, disasters, and endless exasperation. When my husband came home from work that evening, he looked around and playfully asked, "What did you do all day?" Well, I think you can imagine my reaction. Feeling that he—or rather no one—understood what each day was like as a full-time mommy, I replied to my husband's questions like this. "Oh excuse me, my master, how may I serve you? Let me set aside the 100 *%#$% other things that needed to be done right now, so I can clean the scum growing between your toes with my tongue." (I have a slight tendency to get a little mouthy and dramatic with those that I love, but, dammit, I was frustrated.) Afterwards, my heart sank even further. Not only did I feel inadequate and alone; I felt guilty for my outburst. Sadly, these are feelings we mothers experience all too often.

Granted, the home did smell like a frat house after rush week with the nauseating aroma of bleach, air freshener, and beer. Not to mention that I hadn't gotten the kids out of their jammies or combed my hair yet. Dishes covered the counter and the baby was having a fit of the extended case of the five-o-clock fussies. The shoe garden was sprouting at the bottom of the stairs, and a mountain of laundry was waiting for us to scale it, and we had a family of sticky toy lizards residing on our ceiling. I could go on, but I think you get the picture. The house, the kids, and I were in shambles. Still, his good-humored question left me feeling deflated. Was this what mommyhood was like?

After a few hours of wallowing in self-pity while watching the Goldfish crackers swim in the sea of my slightly bluish-white carpet, I started thinking about other moms and their lives. Surely, their days were far more glamorous or, at least, more relaxed than mine. Were they home with their children watching cartoons, or were they sending their kids into a time-out? Were they out starring in a movie or just curled up on the couch watching home videos? Were they running businesses or just running errands? Or perhaps they were sitting in a chair, wallowing in self-pity, looking at the Goldfish crackers swimming in the carpet, wondering the same thing I was.

In an effort to answer these questions, I decided to eschew housework and cooking (two easy choices) as well as sleep (not an easy choice). I started asking my mama-friends to describe their "run of the mill" day. The answers humbled and inspired me. I started to feel less isolated and more connected. I decided to go a step further and asked moms around the world about their days. Would they be willing to let us peer into their lives?

The resounding answer was yes! Their replies highlighted the most mundane of tasks and illuminated the deepest, hauntingly familiar feelings of motherhood.

The end result was MOMMYHOOD DIARIES: LIVING THE CHAOS ONE DAY AT A TIME. It documents an ordinary "day in the life" of moms from all walks of life — rock star moms to stay-at-home moms, CEO moms to work-at-home moms, suburban moms to homeless moms, affluent moms to destitute moms. Through a collection of over 100 day diaries, moms reveal in their own words what a typical day is like for them. Their entries will leave you humbled, inspired, connected and more. Like a reality show on motherhood, we are given the opportunity to voyeuristically peek into the lives of these mothers, as well as to find the common threads that connect us so we can continue learning, living, and loving the chaos of mommyhood.

So, the next time someone asks, "What did you do all day," hand them a copy of this book. Then sit back, relax, and smugly know that you, and your floor of Goldfish, are not alone.

~ In mommyhood and chaos,
Julie Watson Smith

New Beginnings

Be the change you want to see in the world.
~ Mahatma Gandhi

...I'm not a mom yet, but my husband and I are trying to conceive. I already feel like a mom though. I've even bought little outfits for our future baby. My friend told me that there is no other feeling in the world like the first time you see your child. I can't wait to find out if this is true. I can't wait to be a mom!

~ Monica N, 23, Ohio
Anxious mom-to be...someday

12:01 AM Just finished nursing my daughter. I pray I can get just two hours of straight sleep. Sleep deprivation has taken on a whole new meaning. I don't remember ever being this exhausted after pulling all-nighters in college. Of course, I wasn't doing it for five weeks straight either.

~ Susan A, 23, Oregon
Newbie mother of one (age 5 weeks)

I am up to start a brand new day. Today I am excited, because we are supposed to finally have some good weather for more than one day. It has been so cold and depressing in Ohio this winter. That includes the "wonderful" snowfall right before Christmas that left us with snow past our knees as well as the ice storm that caused our power to go out for almost a week. Waking up to the sun shining through my bedroom windows is wonderful.

~ Michelle S, 26, Ohio
Bright mom of two (ages 4 and 2)

6:05 AM I started the morning with my usual mantra. "Today is the first day of the rest of my life. I'm going to make it the best I can." Then, as usual, I fall back asleep with Sarah cuddled in my arm. Life is good, and I'm really going to make today the best of my life!

~ Leah W, 29, Rochester, NY
Optimistic mom of one (age 5)

I took a home pregnancy test this morning, and there was a plus sign on it!! I am so excited!

~ Maria A, 27, Southern California
Soon-to-be mom of one

6:15 AM Coffee. I. need. Coffee. Sweet, glorious coffee.

~ Laurie J, 24, Colorado
Caffeine-addicted mother of one (age 16 months)

7:05 AM There is no way that the children can already be up. Don't they realize that mommy had one too many glasses of wine last night at mom's night out? I have a splitting headache. Agh! I guess my mom was right. Motherhood doesn't stop for anything—especially not a hangover. Oh, how I long for the days before kids when I could sleep until noon, wake up, pour a cup of coffee and crawl back in bed until dinner. Oh well, back to reality.

~ Tiffany S, 28, Southern California
Hung-over mother of two (ages 2 and 9)

7:15 AM I start the morning with my daughter's Blues Clues slippers in my face. She crawled in bed with us again last night. She said she is afraid that the bed bugs are going to get her.

~ Mary S, 29, Wyoming
"Buggy" mother of one (age 4)

Dear Diary,

Today I became a mom. No, I wasn't in the hospital in painful labor. Rather, I spent innumerable hours in the law office signing adoption papers.

~ Sarah P, 42, New York
Committed mother of one (age 6 weeks)

❧

All my life, I've had this dream to act, so I'm finally taking an acting class. Some days I don't know what I'm thinking. I'm a mom, I'm in my thirties, and I live in L.A.—the land of perpetual actors. Even with three strikes against me, I can't help but try. I want to show my baby girl that I can do anything and she can too!

~ Christin P, 32, Southern California
Thespian mother of one (age 22 months)

❧

Dear Diary,

Today is a glorious day. I love being a mom, a wife, a woman.

~ Sara Y, 29, Northern California
Appreciative mom of two (age 4 and 2)

❧

I've been thinking about becoming a foster parent. My husband thinks fostering would be a wonderful thing, but he's worried about the affect on our two children. I think my family could be a positive influence on another child. I'm going to attend a class tonight about fostering. I'm nervous about this new chapter in our life.

~ Natalie H, 34, Northern California
Married mother of two (age 12 and 9)

I'm looking forward to watching my twins grow into the different people that they are. I'm excited to see what new challenges and joys motherhood brings to me when they start to crawl, walk, talk, run, et cetera. I don't think I would trade being a twin mommy for anything in the world!

~ Mary Elizabeth B, 27, Wisconsin
Double-the-fun mom of two (twins, age 9 months)

This morning I woke up with my son in my arms and the man I love laying close against me. Joseph, my husband, got up and gently took our little baby from me, hugged him and changed his diaper. Then I sat next to the window and rocked him in the beautiful rocking chair Joseph got for me, and nursed my gorgeous, perfect little boy. After, we gave him a bath—Joseph is a natural at baby-care; he knows exactly what to do! I took a bunch of photos because I just love his cute tiny naked body! Our little son did wonderfully, enjoying the warm water. We toweled him off and got him dressed and put him down for a nap. He's such a gift, such a treasure! I'm so very happy. It's just the most amazing privilege to finally have him here with us, what an absolute pleasure. Oh, it sounds like he's waking up...I should go see if he's ready to nurse again.

~ Rebecca V, 34, Southern California
Appreciated mother of one (age two weeks)

First Impressions

Paula S, 39, Vermont
The "All-Sports-Mom" of Five

Paula is a married mother of four boys and one newly-adopted daughter (ages 16, 15, 12, 9 and 2). She is devoted to her family's unity, strength, and growth. A former substitute teacher, Paula, also known as the All-Sports Mom, is a columnist, radio talk show co-host, and the author of ***Living in a Locker Room***. When she's not keeping herself busy chatting on the airwaves, penning a new column or developing a new book, she's attending one of the many events her children are involved in through school, church, and sports. A love of culture, music, animals and antiques, Paula is best known for being devoted, sympathetic and loyal. "My family and friends are very important in my life and mean the world to me!"

7:30 AM It's Wednesday morning and I'm wide awake. As I rub my eyes and stretch, it hits me. Today is the day I am going to meet my daughter!

7:31 AM I jump out of bed, which I normally never do, as I am not a morning person, and smile all the way to the bathroom. YES!

7:35 AM I check on my boys. They are all still asleep. I let them stay home from school today as we will be driving from our home in Chelsea, Vermont, to the Logan Airport in Boston, Massachusetts (a three-hour trek), and they will get to meet their new little sister.

7:45 AM I take my shower, humming a tune the whole time. I am so happy. I can hardly believe this day is finally here. I will soon be holding my little girl! I rethink everything that

Tom, my husband, told me the night before on the phone from Guatemala. He said she is just beautiful and he can't wait to bring her home. I am so thrilled that our son, Phillip, who is 12 years old, traveled along on this adoption journey with his Dad to bring his two-year-old Guatemalan sister home. It will be an experience that they will never forget.

8:00 AM I get myself dressed, put on my make-up and blow-dry my hair. Soon my three boys will be waking.

9:00 AM The phone rings. It is our dentist office reminding us of my two older sons, Tony and Nick, check-ups tomorrow afternoon.

9:02 AM My nine-year-old son, Joseph, wakes up and is so excited about our special day. He keeps asking when we are leaving to go to the airport.

9:30 AM My two older boys awake and we have our breakfast. The boys choose cereal, Pop Tarts, and bagels.

9:56 AM I look at my to-do list for the day. Before leaving for the airport I need to start some laundry. I gather it all up, load it in, and hit the wash button. I wonder what my daughter is doing right now at this very moment. I just can't help it; my thoughts keep drifting, thinking of her.

10:21 AM I start my computer and check email. Wow, 120 emails already this morning! I go through my email, deleting some and reading others. I send out my replies. This usually takes a while.

10:57 AM I decide that I am not going to work today. Being a writer, I normally write everyday. Today, I just can't seem to focus. My mind is elsewhere!

11:00 AM I switch the laundry to the dryer. I then wander upstairs to my daughter's newly decorated bedroom. I imagine her there, sitting on her daisy decorated bed happily looking at a book. Everything is ready and waiting for her arrival. I go back down to the kitchen and pack a dinner for us to have on the drive home.

11:25 AM I decide to brush-up on my Spanish and look through our English-Spanish dictionary I have purchased. My husband, Tom, says she has been pointing to different objects and saying words in Spanish, her native tongue.

12:00 Noon We leave in 1 1/2 hours! I get the clothes out of the dryer, fold them and put them all away. My son, Joseph, asks me again when we are leaving for the airport. He is so excited! My two older boys are playing video and computer games down in our rec room of the basement.

12:16 PM The phone rings. Wrong number. I stop and think of my daughter, son and husband. Right now they are flying somewhere over the Atlantic on their way home to us. I look down at my arm. I have goose-bumps.

12:30 PM Time to make lunch. I take a vote. Everyone wants macaroni and cheese today. Easy enough. I also make a cake for my daughter's arrival.

12:59 PM I look at some of the things that I have bought for my daughter. I pick up the journal and begin to write. Someday she will look back and read this special diary that I have written to her.

1:12 PM Time to start packing up the car and making sure that everyone is dressed and ready. As I am packing things into the car, I notice our little girl's car seat that we have already put in the middle seat. For a minute I picture her there smiling up at me.

1:24 PM We leave in half an hour. I remember we need to fill the car with gas on the way. My stomach feels as though it has butterflies.

1:30 PM I check my email one last time for today. There are more well wishes from family and friends.

1:40 PM I take one more walk through our house knowing that in just a few short hours we will have a new addition to our family. I call the boys to get their shoes on and get in the car.

1:45 PM We are off to the Logan Airport. My son, Joseph, waves goodbye to our yellow lab, Charlie, who watches us drive away.

2:01 PM I look at the clock in our car. The plane from Guatemala to Atlanta is just about to land, and then they will board another plane to fly from Atlanta to Boston. I am so nervous and excited that I could burst!

2:39 PM My boys are asking lots and lots of very good questions about their new little sister. I turn the radio down and enjoy our discussion. My guys are wondering what it will be like to have a sister in the house since their mom has always been the only GIRL!

3:14 PM I HOPE SHE LIKES ME.

3:47 PM My youngest keeps asking me how many more minutes until we are at the airport.

3:48 PM Snack time everyone!

4:25 PM My older boys ask how much longer until we are at the airport. Ugh.

4:59 PM We arrive at Logan Airport. YEAH! We park the car and start walking and walking. (It's a huge airport!)

5:11 PM We are in the airport. I look at my watch; we have an hour to kill. My boys don't mind. They are hungry again and head to the food court. Good grief.

5:40 PM I am spending all my money at the Logan Airport! First at the food court, and now we are in a hat shop. I hope I have money left over to pay for parking!

6:02 PM I tell everyone to make a quick potty break...

6:07 PM We check the message board for flights. OH MY GOD! The plane has landed — seven minutes early!

6:08 PM We make a mad dash to Terminal C. What a sight this must be!

6:10 PM My eyes are glued to the area where travelers are exiting from Terminal C. I am shaking. My sons are smiling at me and asking if I am OK.

6:12 PM I see them. I think. Yes, it's them, walking right towards us! I yell out to my son, Nick, to get the camera ready. First, I see my son, Phillip, smiling his adorable smile directly at me. Next, my husband, Tom. He looks so proud. Then I follow his left arm down to his hand that is holding another. There she is, walking along, holding her Daddy's hand, and taking in everything around her. The first thing I notice about my daughter is her beautiful, shiny black hair. Then as they are closer, her big, dark brown eyes meet mine. It is love at first sight. I then feel the tears running down my cheeks. Our wait, over the past two years, has all been so worth it. I smile at her, take her hand and whisper, "Welcome to our family, Anna Grace."

6:24 PM We take lot and lots of pictures right there in the airport.

7:00 PM We head back to Vermont—so anxious to show Anna her new home. She does excellent during the car ride, enjoying her four brothers and even once in a while giving me a friendly smile. It amazes me how sweet and innocent this child really is. In just a matter of minutes, her whole life has changed forever. She will be too young to remember this day, and only have photos to look back on; but for the rest of our family, this has been an experience like no other, and we will always hold dear this special day for our Anna Grace.

And Baby Makes How Many?

Susanna B, 33, Germany
Faith-filled mother of four

Susanna, military wife and mother of four (ages 11, 8, 6, and 17 months), never thought she'd be living the life she has, but after 14 years of being married to her best friend, she is completely content with what she has in life. "Optimism and contentedness comes from trusting that there is a loving God who created me, united me with my husband, created the kids I have and chose me to be their mother, and has my future in His hands. I may not know what I'm doing, but He does."

MIDNIGHT Blessed sleep. The baby, 17 months old, is cutting her bicuspids and hasn't been sleeping too well.

1:30 AM Sure enough, she wakes up for a quick drink of juice and a search for the pacifier she has flung out of her crib. I debate whether to give her a dose of Motrin. I decide to skip it and tuck her in.

3:30 AM Bummer. She's awake again. I should have gone with the Motrin. Now I hoist her downstairs, dig out the medicine syringe, and give her a teaspoon. She takes it good-naturedly and snuggles against my shoulder. I notice on my way up the stairs that the sun is already appearing at the horizon here in Germany. It didn't even set last night until after 10 PM! It will be bright daylight before 5 AM. Hopefully, I will not be awake to see it.

6:30 AM We're up for the day. School was out for the big kids, ages 11, 8 and 6, last week. I'm glad to let them sleep in. My husband has already left for his job as an Army attorney. The baby and I head downstairs for some raisin bread. She has juice, and I pop open a Diet Pepsi—my caffeine of choice.

7:15 AM The big kids are awake! It's a little early, but they are happy to celebrate a summer day. Yesterday we all worked hard to get the house cleaned up after a week's worth of company. Today I have promised they can have a nothing day.

8:00 AM After a massive argument over sniffing noses at the breakfast table—sigh—I suggest everyone spend a little time alone in their rooms. Summer has just started and we've already had too much time together.

8:30 AM I hop in the shower. Everyone is getting along now and the big kids are entertaining the baby. Having kids ten years apart is a fantastic idea!

While showering it occurs to me that we are flying to the United States for a seven-week visit in exactly one week. I have momentary panic when I consider all I have to get done in the next six days. But I remind myself that I have been doing this for the past 14 summers. I am definitely a pro at packing up multiple children and carting them around the world for weeks on end. This is usually done without my soldier husband since he's almost always working while we travel. I know he misses us, but I can't help sometimes thinking he has the easy job.

10:30 AM Husband arrives home to watch the kids while I go to a doctor's appointment. I took a pregnancy test several weeks ago that turned up positive. I've been in denial, but need the details before I head off on my trip. I'm also unwilling to tell anyone about Baby #5 until we know for sure. Most people already think we are crazy to have four kids. Five just seems over the top.

11:30 AM I'm sitting in the office of the same German obstetrician who delivered our first child more than 11 years ago when we were stationed here the first time. He seems as surprised to see me as I am to be here. Everything checks out perfectly. I'm eight weeks along and get to see the heartbeat on the ultrasound. Nothing like seeing an inch-long bundle of beating heart to make it all real. For the first time I feel like it will all be okay.

It seems like déjà vu. Just two years ago we were in shock and denial over the unexpected pregnancy of baby number four. This is somehow less traumatic since she has been such a fun and wonderful addition to the family. Can five really be any more trouble than four?

The only little detail bothering me is the due date. The doctor says 26 January, but I'm calling it 1 February. I am determined to get home for Christmas. It means another trans-Atlantic flight with four kids (never mind being eight months pregnant), but my husband deploys to Iraq in September, and I do not want to be alone here in Germany for the holidays.

The other issue is that he may not be home in time for the birth. I just can't think about that at all right now. What on earth will I do if he's gone? Who will be here to help with the other kids? What will it be like to deliver a child without my right-hand man? I've never even considered that he could NOT be there. I have to trust that God knows what He's doing with this timing. But I look at the calendar and just shake my head.

1:00 PM The house is a mess, and it's hard to ignore it, but I promised no work today. My standards are so different now than they were ten years ago. If I were childless, I would live in a stark loft with shiny surfaces and immaculately organized bookshelves. When I feel especially overwhelmed, I close my eyes and visit my alter ego living in sanitary, well-rested bliss. It's nice. But lonely.

2:00 PM The big kids are still entertaining the baby by wrestling with her on the floor. She already has a black eye from falling off the couch yesterday. She's tough. Now they are screaming and holding their noses because she's filled her diaper. Nothing clears them out of the room faster than a poopy situation. I change her quickly and they come back.

3:15 PM The phone rings and it is my mother-in-law wondering about our schedule when we get to the States. She wants us to stay longer at her place. It's such a challenge to keep everyone happy while we are visiting. I'm exhausted already just thinking about it. I'm also worried about how our families will take the news that we're providing yet another grandchild. They ridiculously spoil the ones we have. Will they feel stretched too thin? I suspect they think we are a little crazy as well.

3:46 PM I cut a slice of fresh bread from our local bakery and get it just right with butter and apricot jam. The baby sniffs it from the other room and comes running. Motherhood will suck the selfishness right out of you, I think, as I watch her inhale every last crumb. I think about cutting another, but realize I'd better serve everyone else first or I'll just end up giving away my slice three more times.

4:35 PM My six-year-old has asked to make microwave popcorn. "Sure," I yell down the stairs. He's done it a dozen times before and knows to set the time to four minutes. About nine minutes later, I smell the burning and run down to see he's forgotten about it and the entire kitchen is smoky. I toss the charred popcorn out the backdoor, throw open all the windows and scold him. "I'm such a dumbhead," he mutters as he walks away. Sigh. I grab him into my lap and soothe him by reminding him that one of the adults living here ruined the first microwave just a few months ago by absent-mindedly putting in a coffee cup with a metal rim. He feels better and hops down to continue playing with his Bionicles.

5:00 PM We had to clear out of the house since the smell of burned butter was so strong. I take a quick stroll with the baby and my eight-year-old. She chats the entire 30 minutes about how much she wants a pony. She wants to know where we're moving next and whether there will be a place to have a pony. Why can't we just move to Texas near her grandparents who have a dozen horses? I wonder why too.

6:30 PM The six of us sit down for a dinner of barbecue chicken. While everyone is eating, we show the kids the ultrasound picture from today and inform them a new sibling is on its way. "Boy, boy, boy!" yells my son. He thinks having three sisters is fundamentally unfair. Having another sister might be more than he can take. They seem excited and immediately start throwing out name suggestions including Junior and Eloise.

8:00 PM I am exhausted and a little nauseous from the pervasive smell of the popcorn. Everyone starts moving toward bedtime, and I'm ready to join them. My husband has cleaned the kitchen (scrubbed the microwave too). He is such a good man.

9:00 PM I'm in bed already reading a little. My husband comes up and stretches across his side. I scratch his head while we catch up on our day and what tomorrow holds. These days we don't do much planning past a day or two. It's easier. There's just too much to think about.

10:00 PM I can't stay awake any longer. The sun is setting and I drift off to sleep hoping that the last dose of Motrin we gave the baby will last a little longer than six hours. Just a few hours of blessed sleep is all I want.

Notes in the Key of Life

Joy R, 47, New York
Rockin' mother of four

Joy is the single mother of four children ages 10 to 15 living in New York. Her life has been filled with new beginnings, and she sees each challenge as an opportunity to express herself artistically. This rock-star mama is the founder and lead singer of the all-original band, Housewives on Prozac (www.housewivesonprozac.com) as well as founder of the nationwide MAMAPALOOZA Festival, dedicated to Mom-Artists everywhere. Featured in print and television around the world, Joy encourages and promotes the creative expressions of moms everywhere!

There are three guitars strewn around the living room. In five minutes the kids will slam through the door, and I'm not ready. I'm never "ready." Life is always bowling me over, and I have no choice but to pick myself up before the next ball hits.

It took me forty-seven years to get here. Twenty to grow up. Thirty to get pregnant. Thirty-seven to finish delivering the last of four kids. Thirty-nine to finish chemotherapy. Forty to start a rock band, and forty-three to have a kidney transplant. I'm tired.

The morning started out rough, and I'm not over it yet.

That's what the guitars are about. I'm trying to turn today's frustration into music. The opening line, over a C chord progression is: 'It's eight o'clock in the morning, and I feel I've lived a thousand years.'

My thirteen-year-old son is curled up on the couch, tears pouring from his eyes, as he clutches his hair and pulls. "I can't go to school."

The diagnosis, 'bi-polar', does nothing to soothe my state of mind. We all have something, some label that can be applied to better categorize and treat us.

I wonder what they'd come up with for a woman who writes songs instead of doing the laundry. Dysfunctional? Non-integrated? Or, just slightly rebellious?

An hour after school, starts the phone rings. My son's asleep in the nurse's office after being partially restrained by the principal.

"I'll call you if you need to come and pick him up," the nurse tells me.

I am wondering which came first — the music or the insanity. Do only crazy people write songs, or does rock and roll invoke the spirit of the self-destructive, manic outcast? Does it affect one's children similarly?

I blame myself, of course.
That's what parents do.

If there's a problem, it must be my fault.

Either the genes, the sometimes angry father, or the fact that after three years in a hospital bed, I decided music was the only thing that could save my life.

It was selfish of me, I know.
And some of the neighbors haven't let me forget it.
There are comments. My family blames me, at least a little.

Songs like, "Eat Your Damn Spaghetti" and "Baby Slave" have turned me into a zealot for creativity. Of any kind. Passion. Lack of conformity. Whatever liberates the soul from crushing banality of the daily grind. It's resulted in a kind of local celebrity status—which means as a mother, I'm up for even closer public scrutiny.

I pick up the guitar and strum another line.

This will be good for the next album.

It's the only thing I seem to be able to control.

Fingers on guitar and the sweet flowing of music straight from heaven through my all-loving, but imperfect heart.

A New Phase

Tracy Lyn M, 35, Canada
Reflective mother of two

Tracy Lyn, a married mother of two (ages 6 and 9), author of ***Mom Management***, and time and life management consultant reflects on the change of having toddlers and preschoolers underfoot to having school age children who are never home. "I really have found that the kids adjusted to this life change much easier than I have. I guess kids are a little more flexible. However, I think that there really is something to the idea that we as moms need to nurture and care for our own feelings as we go through these life altering moments. Next diary piece—puberty!" For more information on Tracy Lyn, visit her at www.mommanagement.com.

As I watched both of children file out of the gym heading towards their classrooms, I realized I was entering a new phase of my life. I have been joking around that I couldn't wait for the moment that I actually had all day everyday to myself. Imagine being able to actually work a seven hour day in seven straight hours rather then in one to three hour spurts—why that seemed like a dream. Yet here it was the day I had looked forward to for a long time and I wasn't sure how to feel. Should I be excited or sad? Should I cry or laugh? So I went grocery shopping!

When I was a stay-at-home mom, I prided myself on never being at home. We were always on the go. Now, I am slowly thinking of creating some plans and routines for myself. I do some traveling for media and presenting, which is great, and the weeks before and after that mean getting ready and catching up. There's no time to worry about being alone then! However, in general, I go to the gym almost every morning.

Sitting and thinking during the rest of the day, it hit me that we, as mothers, have many milestones we go through. Some are very exciting, and some are very difficult. We often are so focused on our children at these times that most of us, including those around us, forget about our own emotions. Watching your children get on the bus for the first time or walk down the aisle at their wedding are incredibly emotion filled days. While the changes children make as they grow are more obvious—baby to toddler to teenager, parents also continue to grow and change throughout life. From the moment a mom finds out she is pregnant, she changes and continues to change. Change is a must, since I'm sure parenting a teen is very different than parenting a baby.

It is very crucial for society to remember that mom and dad are also experiencing strong emotions and stress during these changes. We need to be there to support and encourage the parents as much as we are for our children. Having both lost and then re-discovered my own sense of self when my children were very young, I truly understand how hard these milestones can be on the parents.

Postlogue: "I wrote this piece on the first day of school, and, now, five months later, I am still adjusting. I was excited about those seven hours a day to work. Well, seven hours a day at home alone is long time. I realized that I don't like being home all day...alone. I am actually—gasp—considering a job. "Oh no," the entrepreneur in me says, but I am thinking a contract. Something that allows me to present on life and time management, write, and work with companies on marketing to moms. Something so I don't feel alone."

Birth Day

Holly J, 25, Texas
Brand-Spanking new mom of one

Mom-to-be and new mom all in one day, Holly, mother of one (age 1 day), shared with us the excitement, anxiety, and unadulterated joy of her daughter's birth. "Amazed. Surprised. Scared. Tired. Happy. There just aren't enough words to describe how I feel. I'm overcome by how much love I already feel for this little being. I'm looking forward to being the best mom I can for my little Angela!"

6:30 AM Wake up. Oh my goodness. I feel big, really big. I still have about two weeks to go until my due date. I'm glad–not that I don't want to the baby to arrive—I just really want to finish a few things. Plus I've enjoyed having a little bit of time to myself during the days. I left work a week ago, so I've been enjoying the days by reading and spending time relaxing. All my friends who have kids say that I should take advantage of it now, because, once the baby comes, I won't have time to do anything. I'm sure they are right, but at least I'll have time when the baby sleeps.

6:45 AM Shower and get ready. I have a doctor's appointment at 9:00.

NOON The past few hours have been a whirlwind. It looks like I'm going to be a mom today. Wow! The doctor did a vaginal exam, and I was already 3 cm dilated. He was concerned, because I haven't been feeling the heartbeat as much. He did a non-stress test and said the baby's heart rate was decelerating. He said we should go ahead and induce. I've been crying all morning. I just want the baby to be okay. The doctor said this happens a lot and all the babies are fine. I can't believe today is really the day. I'm going to be a mommy in just a little while. I'm waiting for my husband to get here right now with my overnight bag. After he gets here, they are going to break my water. I'm really scared about everything. I have no idea what to expect. Oh—I better go. Here comes the nurse.

10:07 PM I can't write much. I had a beautiful, perfect baby girl, Angela, an hour ago at 9:02 PM. She weighs 7 pounds

2 ounces and is 19-1/2 inches long. She's perfect. The nurses are still cleaning her up. Labor and delivery went really fast. The doctor said I was made for making babies. Tim, my husband, is calling all our family right now. I can't stop crying. I'm so happy. I kinda feel like my life is going to be brand new now.

Working 9-to-5... and Then Some

The phrase "working mother" is redundant.
~ Jane Sellman

I get to work. I work. I do my job. I go home eight hours later. No biggie.

~ Mary Elizabeth B, 27, Wisconsin
Double-the-fun mom of two (twins, age 9 months)

9:00 AM I'm getting ready to present to the Board of Directors when I notice a big glob of spit-up all over my suit jacket. I'm not so sure about this whole working mom gig.

~ Suzanne P, 28, Alabama
"In need of a dry clean" mom of one (age 7 months)

Dear Diary,

I'm starting a new job today! It's been six years since I left my last job to become a mom. I'm so excited. My little girl started kindergarten about a month ago, so I decided it would be nice to do something else. One of my dreams has always been to paint, so I thought I'd take baby steps and get a job in an arts and craft store. Yeah!

~ Nicole N, 35, New Mexico
Working mom of one (age 6)

3:34 PM I'm nervous. I'm giving my two-week notice to my boss. He's not exactly the happiest man in the world, so I'm scared that he is going to be mad. I don't know why I care, but I do. My heart isn't in my work anymore. After the birth of my second child five months ago, I felt a powerful urge to stay home with them. Okay—deep breath. I can do this. Wish me luck!

~ Donna T, 29, Northern California
"Retiring" mom of two (age 3 and 5 months)

...I'm returning to work next week, and I'm still nursing my daughter. I don't know how to make this work. I work in an "open office," so it isn't as if I can pump at my desk. I could use the bathroom stall, but that seems so cumbersome. I'm finding that work and motherhood aren't always the best combination. I'm sure I'll figure it out, though.

~ Heather S, 34, Indiana
Breastfeeding mother of one (age 4 months)

Today, I got called into my supervisor's office. He said that he was receiving complaints about me leaving at 3:00 each day. I told him, "Yes, I do leave at 3 PM, but only because I arrive at work at by 7 AM and skip my lunch hour." I reminded him that he approved this schedule when I came back to work after my maternity leave. Now he is asking for me to only use this schedule three days a week and have a traditional 8-5 job the other two days. If I didn't like my job so much, I'd probably quit. Instead, I'll need to pray that daycare can keep the kids there a little longer those two days.

~ Angie J, 30, Southern California
Flex-scheduled mom of two (ages 5 and 8 months)

I work full-time as a Quality Validation Consultant for a financial institution. I sell Avon part-time; six months ago I created my own publishing company and started producing a neighborhood directory. But most of all, I'm a full-time mom and significant other to a very nice man. Sometimes I wonder why I'm so darned tired....

~ Tina S, 43, Nevada
Multi-tasking mom of one (age 2)

4:05 PM I started working night shifts a few months ago to save daycare expense for my two children. I'm a single mom, and saving money is important. My mom helps out with the kids at night. She is wonderful with them, and they love her. I feel like I'm being replaced, though. It isn't anything she is doing. It's just that I don't have the energy she has since I'm working at night. I'm so tired in the day that I have no energy to take them to the park. I shouldn't complain, though. My kids know that I love them (I hope). And, in the back of my mind, I know this situation isn't permanent.

~ Rebecca T, 26, Montana
Hard-working mother of two (ages 4 and 3)

❧

A year ago I started working from home. I type resumes, and I type A LOT of reports for college students. I absolutely love doing it. I know I'm not making the salary I was before, but I make enough to put money into the kid's college fund and still have a little money left over for me.

~ Jennifer C, 27, Illinois
Key-tapping mom of two (ages 7 and 5)

❧

In Shape for Motherhood

Lisa D, 33, Southern California
Fit mom of one

"I am the luckiest woman in the world. I LOVE being a mom and am grateful for each moment with my son, and I LOVE my career. But maybe it's not luck. I truly believe that if it's important for you to "have it all" that it can be done. Of course, nothing comes without work and, naturally, lack of sleep," says Lisa, a married mom of one (age 3), and founder of Stroller Strides, one of the fastest growing fitness chains in the United States. Lisa has been featured in several print and television mediums including a recent piece on the *Today*

Show to discuss mom entrepreneurs. A fitness and nutrition enthusiast, Lisa hopes to pass her lifestyle onto her son and upcoming baby. To find out more about Lisa, log onto www.StrollerStrides.com.

5:00 AM   Alarm goes off and I ask myself, "Did I really mean to wake up this early?" The answer is yes, because this is when my "work day" starts so I can still have time with my son. I drag myself down for my much needed cup of coffee and return to my computer to respond to the 100 or so e-mails that have accumulated since I left at 3:00 yesterday.

6:30 AM   "Momma, can I get up?" That is how my son calls out and lets me know he's ready to get up. I feel like I've barely had five minutes to work when, in fact, a full hour has flown by. I cuddle in bed with him and give him a tickle. "Momma, play with me." That's his second sentence of every morning. Not a day goes by that I'm not grateful for the fact that we can go down to play.

7:30 AM   Breakfast is served. I always try to make a nice breakfast for my family. Because my husband works most nights, this is often our "family" meal. With my background in nutrition, it's also impossible for me not to start my family without a balanced meal for the day. Each day Jake asks to watch his videos while we eat and each day I try to explain that meal time is family time and not T.V. time. After breakfast, my husband takes on parent duty. Many people say how they would dislike their husband's working week nights. I actually love it. He gets to spend the first hours of the day with Jake, and it gives me lots of work time.

8:00 AM Phone calls and e-mails.

9-10:00 AM I still teach my Stroller Strides class three days a week. This is truly the best job in the world. I get to teach fitness to new moms and have a great time with the babies. We are outdoors, and it feels as good to me as it does for them.

NOON Lunch. Quick lunch downstairs with Jake and Jason, my husband. Most of the time this is leftovers from the night before.

1-3:00 PM Work Time. Even though I run a fitness business, most of my work takes place at a desk. I'm either responding to e-mails or on the phone with licensees, clients, and sponsors. I love my work, so it never feels like a chore. Because my work hours are less than the average 9 to 5, each minute is precious. Emails and calls are kept brief, so that I can pile through it.

3:00 PM I hear "Momma, can I get up?" for the second time of the day. This time, my son is waking from his nap that his Daddy put him down for two hours earlier. Yes, I know I'm blessed to have such a good sleeper! Wish me luck on the second child. From here through bed time, we have playdates, gymnastics, run errands, and all the other things that most mommies do. Jacob and I have dinner together at 6:00 PM; I give him a bath at 6:30 PM and by 7:30 PM he's off to bed.

7:30-9:00 PM Work time again. I complete any loose ends from the day and set my office up for the next day. I always recommend having coffee pre-set, desk cleared, etc., so you can start your day fresh.

9:00 PM Collapse into bed! I try to read a little bit each night, but admittedly it may be while watching some pathetic reality show.

P.S. Hope you didn't notice that I didn't shower in the day. I always manage to get it in somewhere, although it's often when Jake is bathing as well!

Juggling Act

Carey F, 31, Southern California
"Dealing with it" mother of one

Carey, newly pregnant with her second child and a married mother of one (age two), constantly juggles her responsibilities, desires and dreams. "I am a very determined person that values family, friends, and hard work. I thrive in social surroundings and have to force myself to take a step back and relax. I thoroughly enjoy and respect my career."

5:15 AM Alex is crying out for us. We really, really don't want to get him. He was up for an hour around midnight. Totally regressing! After our Hawaii trip a few weeks ago, bed-time/sleeping have become a struggle. We should hold firm. I'm so exhausted!

5:20 AM I get him and bring him to bed. My husband, Chris has been working ridiculous hours and I know he needs sleep, too. Oh, well. I need to get up anyway and get ready for work. Another day at the crack of dawn. I try to quietly get ready without waking Chris or Alex. These darned new houses with no door to the bathroom!

6:00 AM Making coffee for Chris, Alex's lunch, taking the dogs out for their walk and grabbing something for me to eat. Yesterday was a really rough day. I'm six-and-a-half weeks pregnant. No one really knows yet, so I'm silently suffering. Last pregnancy, I wasn't really sick at all. I'm really hoping yesterday was a fluke. I was so queasy all day!

6:20 AM On the road. In the car, I listen to NPR, trying to stay awake. Although I know our schedules have been crazy, I've been feeling overwhelmed with the prospect of keeping our house clean, child fed, work done, etc. I'm dead center in a discussion in my mind about how even though I know my husband works a lot and has to do so, I can't do this alone. Last pregnancy, I slept every day after work from 5:30 PM on, just waking up to eat dinner. This time, no dice. Plus, I live in a world where there are activities for my son and me EVERY DAY should I choose them. Many neighbors/friends are stay-at-home moms that have fully scheduled their days with crafts, story hours, gymnastics, errand running, etc. I know Alex gets a lot of that at his curriculum-oriented daycare, but still...I know I could always do more. And yes, it's much more than what our parents did for us, but I can't help but feel guilty that I'm not enhancing his life more.

6:40 AM Daily cell phone call to Mom on my way to work. We chat daily while I drive. She knows more about me than anyone else, and vice versa, so we're good sounding boards for each other. Yesterday when we talked in the afternoon, I was very cranky. I'm trying to be better today. I'm so exhausted, I say. I am venting my frustration about how I don't know if I can do it all. She reminds me that when she was pregnant with her second, she quit her job. She also says that I need more help. We discuss how nice it would be, but how difficult it will be to do. It's interesting. I'm not sure that, if I were to stay at home full time, I would feel less overwhelmed. If I'm not sleeping right now, anything else seems like too much. Oh, the joys of the first trimester with a toddler. I laugh at how all baby and pregnancy books are geared toward your first child. How am I going to nap and take care of myself this time?

7:00 AM Get to work. I would kill for a cup of coffee. Things have been hectic at work. There are major things going on both behind the scenes and out front that may seriously affect my future here. I have such a great set up now...if things change as I think they will, things could be very different for me. In a way, the opportunities seem great, but do I want more opportunities, or have I already bitten off more than I can chew?

8:30 AM My daily morning check-in with Chris. How was Alex this morning? Did you have a good morning? Did he eat his breakfast? Did he cry when you dropped him off? It helps me when I can't be there. I hate it when I put him to bed at night and I say "see you in the morning," it isn't really true, but it's been our ritual since he was a baby, and we'll do it forever, I think. He's so close to his daddy though. I'm so lucky. Unless sick or hurt, he really prefers either one of us. He goes through some phases, but it's nice to have a 50/50 parent, at least when Chris is home.

11:45 AM Starving. Always starving these days. Should I a) return library books, b) run to Target for miscellaneous things, c) go to Miramar Lake with a sandwich and veg out, or d) take the first offer that comes inviting me to go out to lunch? I almost always do the latter. Of course, that just postpones my errands for later in the day, when between the traffic and time crunch to pick up Alex, I'm losing my mind!

3:00 PM End of day, time to hit the road. My drive in the afternoon takes me almost an hour on Interstate 15, but much quicker than Interstate 5. I never really thought I'd get used to the commute, but I have. Our decision to move 45 minutes away from my job was a smart one, though. My husband, an attorney, tends to work crazy hours. We sacrificed a few hours of my part-time workday to allow him to get home before Alex goes to bed. We tried for a place more central, but they all seemed to be out of our price range. It helps that Chris takes Alex to daycare, but my day tends to feel very long, especially pregnant. Our decision to move, along with the decision for me to work part-time, has been very fulfilling. It can be difficult, but we think we'll keep doing it until it stops working.

3:45 PM Picking up Alex from his daycare. He's on the playground and sees my car when I pull in the driveway. His face lights up and he runs to the gate. After signing him out and picking up his belongings, I go out to collect him from the playground. Some days he comes right over, others he stays to show off a bit. He has special girlfriends at school, Reagan and Jessica, that he must say goodbye to first.

4:15 PM We're home. After letting the dogs out, we spend some time in the backyard: baseball, riding bikes, playing in the water table. It's the best time of day—just Mommy and Alex. We have snacks, play with the train set, and I attempt to keep Alex occupied while I start dinner. Some days of the week are more crazy than others. Monday afternoons are playgroup, Wednesday is music class, and at least one day we try to go to the water feature at the park. I try to make the most of my afternoons.

6:30 PM Daddy's home! Now the whirlwind of dinner, playing, bath and bedtime starts. Tomorrow is Friday, which is also my day off. By Thursday evening, I'm so ready for it! Friday is such a great day. Besides errands, we go to Stroller Strides fitness class, playgroup, and often have lunch with daddy. It's been the only way I could justify working at all. I have so many special times on Fridays. I still see my old playgroup from down in San Diego occasionally, too.

8:30 PM Alex is down for the night. When I'm not pregnant, Chris and I visit, eat snacks and watch TV together. Maybe he or I will have brought some work home, but usually it's nice couple downtime. Now that I AM pregnant, I drift off to sleep on the couch from 9-10, when Chris puts me to bed. He's pretty patient about his MIA wife, since he now knows what to expect.

This diary truly reflects a typical day in my life. I tend to carry stress with me and not let things go, but, since I've become a mom, I realize how important it is to work on it. I have an amazing support group of friends and family that gets me through when I've overcommitted myself. I believe I am a better person for my family AND my career. Environmental and city planning change the world professionally; and I change my immediate world personally. I am grateful to be given the opportunities I have and will work daily to remind myself of that.

Working Girl

Amy G, 34, Southern California
Aspiring mother of two

A former teacher, Amy, now a stay-at-home mom of two (ages 2 and 4 months) living in Southern California, entered the world of child modeling and casting after the birth of her first child. "After several people stopped me and said, 'you have a Gerber,' I decided to take plunge and sent some pictures to a local modeling agency. They called me the very next day!" Her children have graced the pages of many catalogs and magazines including *Parenting*, Disney, Macy's and more. "My kids' health and happiness always come first. I'm not a stage mom. As long it is fun for us, we'll keep doing what we are doing. I actually find it more difficult to retain my individuality while becoming a wife, mother and, of course, a friend.

Today is my daughter Kate's first casting call. It is an open casting for Itty Bitty Babies from 10 AM until noon. That is all I know. I have heard of the company. It is nobody huge, but I know they make baby carriers and infant toys. They often use multi-ethnic-looking babies, so our prospects aren't great considering Kate is very white with blue eyes, but you never know. My son, Jack had a casting with them when he was little. Actually he was too big for what they were looking for—c'est la vie. So, no, he didn't get the job.

As I learned with Jack, timing is important in casting calls. You want the baby happy and awake. That means he or she can't be hungry causing them to not be too happy. But if the baby has eaten too recently, she might spit up. That's not too cute. Thankfully, she wakes up at 7:00 AM which should put us on a perfect schedule. She eats when she wakes up and won't be due to eat again until 11:00 AM.

The plan is for her to eat, play for a couple hours, and then she'll nap as we drive down to the casting, which, thankfully, is local. Usually it's about a two-hour drive up to Los Angeles. This one is in San Diego. With traffic, it should take about a half hour. If I'm there right when it starts, we should be in and out quickly, and I'll have time to get Jack to his preschool readiness class by 10:30 AM.

This casting will be different than the ones I've been on with Jack, since I'll now have two kids with me. I need to make sure I have a way to make just-turned-two Jack behave so that I can focus my attention on Kate. So, in the diaper bag I pack Elmo fruit chews, a few Hot Wheels, a pop-up book, and a sippy cup with carrot juice, and, oh yeah, a prayer that he does behave.

Now... what does Kate wear? Her agent says solids are best, but I don't have anything solid that is both cute and clean. I opt for a simple floral dress in a blue that matches her eyes and a floppy hat. Bald babies look better in hats. A bib around her neck to keep any spit-up or drool off the dress, and we're off.

As we pull into the parking lot, I see a few other doting parents. Usually I only see other moms, but this time there is a couple. It's obvious this is their only child, seeing the way they so carefully remove the infant carrier so as not to jostle their precious cargo. The two of them together snap the carrier into the stroller. Meanwhile I have Kate's infant carrier in the crook of my elbow as I swing Jack onto my available hip. Thank goodness for automatic doors on my van! We head in.

As we sign in, I size up the competition. Uh oh—twins. I hear the mom telling the casting director "You get two for the price of one." My only consolation is that they aren't nearly as cute as my Kate. Although, I must admit that they come pretty close. That's one thing with these auditions—there are so many cute babies. I guess that's why they're all models. What's amazing to me is how different they look: some with hair, darker skin, chubbier. The common denominator they share, though, is that they are all cute. I have to remind myself that if Kate doesn't get this job that the company must be looking for something different.

Thankfully there are some toys out so Jack goes to town exploring infant toys (always a novelty) while a woman named Amy comes over to Kate. Kate returns Amy's smiles and hellos with a whole body smile. Amy helps Kate into the front carrier of a model who obviously didn't just give birth to this child, because her stomach is far too flat. A Polaroid is taken. "Thank you for coming, we'll let you know next week."

I help myself to the complimentary water bottle, granola bars, and fruit chews (don't want to leave empty-handed), I pack up the kids and go. I think we were there for all of five minutes. Like I said, at least this one was local. You don't get paid for casting calls.

The kids are loaded back into the van, and we're off to Jack's pre-school readiness class. We're trying to see if he's ready for pre-school. We walk in the door just as circle time is beginning. Kate is starving by this point, so I sit at the side of the room to nurse her as Jack decides he'd rather go play with puzzles than sit at circle time. If my boob wasn't hanging out, I'd grab him. But not wanting to expose myself to all these people, Kate gets food, and Jack gets to play. I'm thinking Jack is not quite ready for preschool. Maybe we'll try again in a few months.

Home for lunch: quesadilla on a whole wheat tortilla, fresh fruit and carrot juice. I'm so glad at least one of eats healthy. Pretty soon Jack'll realize that my quesadilla is on a white tortilla and fried in butter served with chips and a Pepsi. Until then...do you think this is why I still have 15 pounds to go to get back to my pre-pregnancy weight? Hmmm....

It is now 1:15 PM, and Jack is down for his nap. Kate is mercifully asleep as well. I'm not sure what to do with myself. Both kids napping at the same time! Do I indulge myself by sitting in the sun with my latest book, or do I catch up on sorting through Kate's drawers? To her closet I go. She's almost out of 0-3 months clothes, but not quite into 3-6 months clothes. It's such a nightmare for me. I hate folding those itty bitty clothes. If I try to do this while Jack is awake, he inevitably takes the clothes out of the "Girl 0-3" box and puts them in the laundry basket, or who knows where. Jack, the anti-helper, strikes again.

Twenty minutes into this chore I hear whimpers. Please go back to sleep, Kate! It quiets down. Hooray! I continue sorting. No, guess not. She's officially crying. Maybe she'd like to sit in her bouncy seat and watch me sort through her drawers? One can hope.

Purposefully Driven

Kathleen H, 34, Southern California
Volunteering mother of two

Kathleen is the married mother of two (ages 3 and 22 months) living in San Diego. A former civil engineer, she now takes pride in being a full-time mom and active volunteer helping to improve drinking water in Mexico. She encourages others to find the rewards in volunteering. "The world would be a better place with more volunteer moms!"

6:45 AM My wake-up call is before 7 AM as Clifford the Big Red Dog is on the TV. My husband, plopping our 22-month-old and three-year-old on my bed, wakes me up as one sits on my leg. Another day begins. Daddy goes to work. The kids are awake. They watch ten minutes of TV, and they are raring to go. Fortunately it is the last day of my period; however, my body still aches. It is amazing how PMS can be ten times worse when you have kids. It starts out several days before you even get your period. I swear, on those days my coping skills are severely limited. I imagine the kids as nothing but monsters set out to make my life miserable. Fortunately, I realize quickly that it is just the PMS talking. Karl, my son, has found some blue Chapstick and is sticking his finger in it. I know this as Anna, my daughter, is reporting to me that he is wiping it on the new bed sheets. I try to take it from him; however, he clinches and says no. I negotiate by asking to put the lid on and let's go put it back. Amazingly he does that.

I jump in the shower and hear the kids playing, fighting and crying all within the quick seven minutes. Then they are fighting with the door. Karl wants it open, and Anna wants it closed. Settled by mom, as I say, very sternly, "Nobody touches it." I just know it is a disaster waiting to happen, doors with fingers smashed. Don't they know disaster is lingering.

The kids eagerly want to go downstairs for breakfast. It is 7:30 AM; Karl wants me to carry him downstairs. I swear he is 30 pounds. I resist, saving my back and holding his hand as he goes down like a big boy. Being the short-order cook I am I rattle off the breakfast menu: yogurt and granola, oatmeal, or pancakes. They want yogurt and granola. My daughter doesn't want the orange spoon I gave her (the one I put in her yogurt). It's the first of many dirty dishes today which daddy is so wonderful to help out with around here. She starts to whimper, pout, and cry. I begin to explain to her that it is fine and to stop being a baby. Then I give in. "Pick your battles," 'they' say. I get another spoon, a green one, and now she is happy. This attitude is so unlike her, or is it me and my PMS?

What should I eat? A protein shake or some toast? Still struggling to lose the pounds that I have acquired through life. Too many years of college, work in front to a computer and now life of snacks and kids. Soon they will both be in pre-school (just a few months away), and I will have some time for myself; albeit only two-and-a-half hours a day.

8:00 AM I mix a protein shake and remind myself that it isn't all about me now. I hand the kids their vitamins. I mop up the yogurt from my son's sleep shirt, wipe it from the floor, and clean off his cup. I can't wait 'til he is not as messy, like his sister.

Time to get the kids cleaned up. Today is Tuesday, off to Ms. Nancy's class for Anna. Two and a half hours with only one child—a break! We need to drop off Anna at pre-school at 9:00 AM.

My head is hurting; neck is sore, after-effects of a bad period, ibuprofen for me. Wish I could sleep, but no rest for mommy. Lots to do today.

8:20 AM First poopy diaper for Karl. Thank goodness Anna is potty-trained; however, Karl doesn't seem the least bit interested in becoming potty-trained. I thought the second one would come easily, naturally, soon; of course, he isn't even two yet. Fortunately, Anna is a big help, getting diaper wipes when mommy asks, getting her own socks, and taking off her clothes. It is great when they get older. Having my kids close in age was crazy, 17 months apart, but it has kept me very busy, still does. However, I wanted to get it all done with having kids and wanted them close.

8:30 AM Kids set. Time for mommy—make-up and a little bit of a blow-dry.

8:45 AM Scramble to get out the door. The infamous hollering of the "car-ride" gets them moving. They love going places. Thank goodness!

9:00 AM Take Anna to Ms. Nancy's class. Talk to a few fellow moms. Said "hi" to one that I met at scrapbook might a couple of weeks ago. Chatted with another who did pre-natal yoga with me when I was pregnant with Anna. It is amazing to me how small the world is and how all these people are tied to me via having a baby. Karl loves Anna's class and doesn't want to leave. But after a moment of hesitation, we are off.

9:20 AM Off to Coronado to meet with a mom that I met who is a consultant to scrapbook supplies. She is also a Stroller Stride teacher, which I did some time ago for exercise, until I had two kids and that became unmanageable. Keeping two kids happy in a stroller—one newborn and one 17-months-old for an hour—it's just not happening.

9:45 AM At Coronado Park, Karl goes up and down the slide a few times and then ventures to the more dangerous play areas. He climbs up and up, and then I go and get him down. He gets bored and wants snacks. We get in the car. Off to the grocery store for some fruit and veggies. Karl likes shopping and helping mom. Then we stop at a local resale store to look for a leotard for Anna. She just started gymnastics class two weeks ago and really likes it. She is so cute. No such luck at this store, and I try to pry the toys from my son's hands as we walk out.

11:15 AM Already time to pick up Anna. Saw a mom in the parking lot and chatted about SUV's and gas prices. Picked up Anna; Karl didn't want to leave and started pulling down all the toys, especially the cars. Finally, we made it to the car, and over to another resale store. The kids play in a play area while I shop. Found several leotards, much cheaper than new. Anna informs me while I am shopping that she needs to go potty and that I better have some diaper wipes handy. I take both kids to the back, and, when I pick up Karl, he is stinky too. But the diapers are in the car so he is going to have to wait and wait and wait. Of course he wants to go through the boxes in the back, and it is dangerous. He is screaming, Anna is singing, and mom is sweating. I take the leotard and purchase it. Anna is done, and Karl is still not happy. Quickly retrieved some vanilla wafers, and Karl is happy. I change his diaper. At home, I make the kids some lunch, and then they fight over the Sit and Spin. Then it is naptime.

1:00 PM Karl is sleeping.

1:10 PM Anna is sleeping

1:11 PM Mommy is on the couch watching her soap. Thank goodness for digital video recorders. I still have a headache and neckache. And I still need to get ready for tonight's board meeting. Tonight's board meeting is my volunteer group, Aqualink (www.aqualink.org), a non-profit organization that provides technical assistance to communities in Mexico for safe drinking water. I am currently president. We recently got an EPA grant to help indigenous communities south of the border in evaluating their current water systems. We have board meetings once a month and fields trips as necessary. This is all volunteer work, free technical assistance, that I do in the evenings, weekends, and when the kids are in bed. Just now, I got a call from a fellow member who needs some information emailed to him. Of course, I am sending it to him, but the server is "busy." It looks like work is at a halt. I enjoy my volunteer work; it is great that I have an outlet to use my other occupation, civil engineer. Thankfully, it is rewarding, stimulating, and keeps my feet in the work force in the event that I go back to "work." I find that my current work, my kids, keeps me busy, fulfilled and happy. I love my kids.

2:15 PM Kids still sleeping. Better vacuum and pick things up around the house. Thank goodness that my kids are good sleepers. I swear that is the only thing that keeps me sane is the peace at naptime and when the kids go down for the evening by 7:30 PM. I have been pretty strict on the naptime and nighttime schedules, and, fortunately, my kids have obliged. But I believe consistency is the key, and it prevents meltdowns too. A tired kid is a crabby, whiny kid.

3:00 PM Vacuumed, mopped, and straightened the house (which just means I put toys away). Phone call regarding home equity loan and financing. Discussed as we are going to need a new car soon, and it would be so nice to have the third row of seats, but is it worth $30,000? So hard to not buy everything you want in today's world, especially on one income. So tempted.

3:15 PM Karl is up and hungry—peanut butter and jelly sandwiches, pretzels, and water. Now he is outside playing in the water he found from running the sprinklers this morning, and he's having fun. Opened Anna's door and told her to get up when she is ready and to come downstairs.

4:00 PM Tried to call Sacramento to talk to someone regarding Aqualink's tax I.D., got switched around and put on hold.

4:05 PM Ordered two pizzas and began to make salad.

Looks like we will have a group of 14 people, 10 members and four guests. I hope the kids behave well during the meeting. It is a challenge since daddy is a member, but he also assists with the children since I am president and running the meeting.

5:00 PM Dad is home cleaning the kids and changing them into their sleepers, while I have some time to change clothes, brush hair, freshen make-up, get a bit professional looking from sweats to jeans. Fortunately, I have the greatest husband. He has a great job and brings home plenty of money to keep us happy. He is a wonderful father and can do lots of domestic things around the house. He has been taking care of these kids right along the side of me from day one and is really good at it. I have no qualms about leaving the kids with him. Of course, when I do leave them with him for more than several hours, he does complain of an occasional headache. Fortunately, I don't have a headache any more. Dad picked up the pizzas, wrong order. I call the pizza company to make sure they didn't overcharge me. Apparently, they didn't. They just gave us the wrong size. Argh. Just when everything is going smoothly, something goes wrong. So, I make more salad.

5:30 PM People are now coming over. We're eating dinner. The kids are happy. Everything is fine.

6:00 PM Meeting started. The kids are watching a video. All is going fine. I enjoy the people in my group. We talk about water projects in Mexico, working with EPA, what we need to do how we are going to accomplish it, and who is going to do what. I sometimes become a control freak and want to do everything; however, I am learning to delegate, and it also gives the members a sense of importance in the group, which they are! Karl keeps coming into the dining room and calling my name. Daddy lets him come to me, and I pick him up and onto my lap. Well, of course, he wants me; he has a poopy diaper! I quickly call dad and hand Karl to him. It is amazing how dads can't ever detect the smell of a poopy diaper but mom's can smell them a mile away! I can't wait 'til I get that boy potty-trained, which I think is the most difficult challenge in these toddler years. I thought my daughter was going to drive me crazy. Every step we took forward, the following week we would go two steps back. It was the ultimate challenge, but I can safely say, she is very well-trained now. Thank goodness.

7:00 PM Daddy takes the kids to bed. They say good night to all the people. They are so cute and such good kids.

7:45 PM The meeting is over.

8:00 PM I talk with one of the members discussing the budget for our project. He is the designated project coordinator, but he wants to split the work and share the funds fifty-fifty. I am flattered, and think, "Oh wow, my own schedule and get some money too." However, we are talking peanuts compared to my last job. It isn't that we aren't making an income since my daughter was born over three years ago. I can't say that money isn't important; it is a necessity. However, the sacrifice I made to stay home with my kids has been invaluable. To some people, I may look crazy to give up $75,000 a year to be what they think I am—a full-time babysitter. But I know, my husband knows, my extended family knows, and practically everyone else who will admit it knows that there is nothing more special than being a full-time mom to your kids. No one can love your kids more than you do. No one will take care of your kids like you would. No one values your kids like you do. I read an article the other day and there was a quote about raising kids and it said, "There may be second chances in jobs, but not in raising kids."

9:00 PM Watch the rest of my soap.

9:30 PM Check email. Return email to my playgroup saying we will make it to Thursday playgroup at Kayleah's house. Send email to EPA regarding grant.

10:15 PM Go upstairs to bedroom, change clothes, wash face, and brush teeth. Talk with husband.

11:00 PM Go to bed.

6:00 AM Another morning. My son is crying for mama, unusually early and a sad cry. Maybe he isn't feeling well or maybe he is teething. I think he has four teeth coming in at one time. But I am still tired; maybe he will lie and cuddle with me in bed. Success! He is cuddled with me in bed while daddy is getting ready for work. I doze off with my baby in my arms. Daddy wakes me up with a kiss good-bye. It is almost 7:00 AM Karl smiles at daddy with this big grin. Daddy smiles back. Anna is calling from her room and is brought in to join us on the bed as we all watch Zooboomafoo on PBS as I slowly wake up for, as my godmother would say, another wonderful, exciting day in Kathyland.

School Daze, Summer Craze

Education's purpose is to replace an empty mind with an open one.
~Malcolm Forbes

I'm spending the day trying to get my son on preschool waiting lists. This is ridiculous. He's only 18 months.

~ Trish H, 27, Southern California
Single mother of one (age 18 months)

I've decided to go back to school. I just celebrated my 50th birthday. I always said one day I'd go back and get a degree. This year I'm going to just do it.

~ Stacy S, 50, North Dakota
Divorced mother of two (ages 14 and 16)

My husband's job requires us to move a lot. We are now living in France. My son is in first grade at an all-French school. He's having a really difficult time reading. Luckily my husband speaks and writes French fluently (he grew up here). I, on the other hand, speak just enough French to get along here. I wish my husband wouldn't push my son into this school. I think he'd do much better in an immersion school that teaches both English and French. This is causing even more stress in our lives.

~ Margorie W, 32, France
Mother of two (ages 6 and 3)

My son's life is taking over our house. Let's see what this week looks like: karate, a play, a book report due, school Harvest Festival, a science project, a math test, a spelling test, school photos—and he just outgrew his gym shoes. Agh! How do other moms handle all this?

~ Lisa M, 26, Ohio
Harried mother of one (age 8)

Preschool graduation is tomorrow. I can't believe my little girl is going to kindergarten after the summer. I'm a little relieved to be done with preschool, though. I never felt like I fit in with the other moms. It was just like high school again with all the cliques. I hope it gets better with both parents and kids once we are in elementary school

~ Tish M, 32, Southern California
Bittersweet mother of two (ages 5 and 1)

I just found out that my son hit another kid at school today. He's four-and-a-half, but his preschool teacher made it sound like he's a mass criminal. Give me a break. I'm not condoning his behavior, but isn't this what preschoolers do?

~ Michele K, 24, Arizona
"Knock-out" mom of one (age 4)

...I'm praying that my son gets into the charter school just across the street from us. He's starting kindergarten soon, and don't want my son in a large school. I've toyed with the idea of homeschooling. I just don't know, though. Being a parent is tough. Every decision I make affects the outcome of their life.

~ Andrea R, 28, Colorado
Soon-to-have-a-kindergartner mom of one (age 5)

Yeah! My daughter just won the weekly spelling bee! I'm so proud of her. She has struggled with much of her coursework, but she really put so much effort into studying this week. I keep telling her that there is nothing she can't do. I'm so proud. I'm just bursting at the seams!

~ Cathy G, 36, Idaho
Beaming mom of three (ages 9, 8, and 3)

❧

It's official. My children are now smarter than me.

~ Deidre L, 41, Michigan
Separated mom of two (ages 14 and 10)

❧

My "baby" is graduating from high school in a few weeks. It seems like it was just yesterday that I was changing his diapers, and now he'll be heading off to college in a few months. Wow! I never thought this day would come.

~ Crystal F, 52, Minnesota
Awed mom of three (ages 23, 19 and 17)

❧

School's in Session

Sami B, 34, Maryland
Educating mom of four

Sami, a married mother of four children (ages 9, 7, 5 and 3) says, "I am a mom, homeschooler and nurturer. I completely enjoy the complexity, as well as the simplicity of motherhood...I believe very strongly in being the best I can be at whatever it is I set out to do, and I feel that all moms should take their positions as such. Nothing is more important than the path I set my children's feet upon. As important as it is to be 'Mommy', it is as important to be 'Sami.' I cherish this time of my life!"

I am pulled out of a jumbled dream by the sound of a slamming door. I reach for the remote under my pillow and point it at the TV, checking the time. 7:38 AM. Too early. I march into the hallway, exhausted after only four hours of sleep, to find the source of the noise. The door slams again, the culprit giggles from the other side. I reach the door and open it to find my three young sons in varied gymnastic positions around their small room. The middle son, Dakota, five, hangs upside down from the bunk bed. As I beg for another hour of quiet, my youngest son, Julian, 3, runs to greet me with a kiss and a sweet sun-like smile. I hug him and explain, AGAIN, that Daddy got home from work at 3 AM, therefore, the need for quiet. The boys climb back onto their beds with various books and toys, and I head back to bed. Sometimes there is sleep; usually there is more door slamming and giggles.

By 9 AM our homeschooling household of six is full of energy and movement. Daddy leaves at 1 PM, so our mornings are packed with chores, activity, planning and conversation. Running a household of six—a CLEAN household of six—requires help from everyone. The older children, Skyler, 9, and Jordan, 7, are a big help. Skyler acts like a doting big sister (which sometimes seems more like a drill sergeant), and helps with breakfast, getting the youngest dressed, and keeping the house dust-free. Jordan, our oldest son, carries down loads of laundry, puts away his clean "digs," and works at keeping our kitchen floor "crunch" free. I start most days by throwing in laundry, booting the computer, and drinking a Pepsi—my only vice. If the morning goes well, I manage a workout. As you may imagine, trying to do yoga while having four children around is a real challenge. Regular exercise is important in my life as a homeschooling mom of many. It is a job that requires an upbeat attitude and much energy. After a quick shower, I spend a few moments alone, as I do each morning, before heading down to my children. Some mornings, during rough times, I find myself thinking, "This is what you do, this is who you are..." a sort of mantra to get myself motivated; most other days, I just go with the flow and really enjoy the freedom of homeschooling.

It's 11:30 AM and I am cooking "supper". This is one of the greatest challenges to our schedule. For many years we were a family with a pretty regular schedule. This spring, a new job for my husband led us to a whole new way of living. I now find myself planning "supper" well before breakfast is done. We usually eat our largest meal of the day before my husband leaves for work, and he takes leftovers for dinnertime. My husband takes some time to explore our backyard gardens with the younger children while I prepare pasta, garlic bread and salad. Dakota, our wild five-year-old, brings me freshly picked basil from his plant in the vegetable garden and eagerly tells me all about the baby-sized cucumbers and tomatoes he saw growing there. He races back outside to help water the bounty, slamming yet another door as he goes!

My daughter enters the kitchen with an armload of laundry and announces that her brother needs to fold it since it belongs to him. Jordan puts his Playmobile knights aside, grabs the clothing and heads to his room, sticking his tongue out at his sister as he goes. Skyler yells something goofy after him and starts to set the table for lunch. I use the few minutes of peace and quiet to ask about her English assignments for the week. She finishes with the table and brings her books to the table, showing me the completed work, going over the difficult problems, asking questions. The two younger children come tearing up the staircase from the playroom excited to see a police car as it rushes by the house, siren almost as loud as their shrieks of joy. My head is full of a million ideas, a million thoughts, and a million things to do. I stir the pasta sauce, check the garlic bread, and begin to plan my day out mentally as I stare into the swirls of steam rising from the boiling rotini. I then realize it's Library Day, and many items are due. I rinse the pasta, remove the bread and rally up the oldest children for a wretched chore: Locating and stacking the library books!

As a homeschooling family, we utilize our county's library system quite well. Sometimes we have almost 200 resources out, all due back at different times. We consider ourselves lucky homeschoolers as well. Our county offers learning toys, storytime packages, drive-thru windows, tons of learning videos, language tapes, brand new DVDs and free classes. For this, we are so very grateful. It is also our reason for so many visits!!

Today the children hunt down several "fun" videos, arguing over who left which movie where. I remind them that videos are privileges and should be treated as such. Soon the videos and books are piled near the front door ready to be returned. We sit down to enjoy our "supper" with daddy, laughing, joking, and sharing our plans for the day with him before he leaves for work. After eating, daddy prepares to leave, and we all work to get the kitchen cleaned up.

At 1:30 PM, our day truly begins. The children are out front, having chased daddy up the street, waving frantically as he drove from sight. We usually hang out front for awhile, discussing our plans for the day, deciding our schedule. Sometimes we decide to run errands, usually to the library and Wal-Mart. Sometimes we stay out and play. Today we decide to get started with lessons, as we have ballet on the schedule before dinnertime. The older children get their school supplies, books, and workbooks off the shelves of our schoolroom and look over their assignment printout for the day. The younger boys head into the playroom to watch a video; occasionally one of them may nap. They spend the next hour watching a "Bug City" video, and "There Goes a Truck", while I read to the older children. Our topic today is People of Northern Europe 500BC, and the kids listen, fascinated. They love Celtic lore, Stonehenge and magic, and these pages were anticipated eagerly. I complete our reading for the day, and we set about working on mapping out Northern Europe and preparing narrative pages for our history notebooks. My daughter works on beautiful illustrations from our reading, and my son looks up further information in library books. As the children wrap up history, I go over concepts of grammar and writing with them individually, and they set about their language arts work independently. If extra help is needed, I work with that child, while the other does free reading, which is required daily. As we are wrapping up those subjects, the little ones appear, looking for snacks! I ask them for just a bit more quiet time and they ask to "do school". I pull out their workbooks and crayons and they begin to work. Dakota traces the letter "H" over and over in green crayon while

Julian points at a sheet of paper, saying everyone's name, as if he is reading. I walk over to him and see that the paper is, indeed, a printout of everyone's name in our family, and he is correct! He points to another word on the sheet and yells, "Snoopy!" I kiss his head and wonder if he's memorized the list. I show him three new words: car, van, dog. I read each one twice then leave him looking at the words, tracing the letters with his finger, slowly saying them one by one, "car...van...dog." I have no doubt that he will recognize them tomorrow. Julian is three and on his way to reading. Dakota sits with his crayons now sorted into very straight, perfectly aligned piles. I watch him move one from a pile and move it to another, making truck noises all the while. I sit next to him. He looks up with a sly smile and says "five crayons take away three crayons is two crayons." I ask how many he has in the pile to which he added these three crayons and watch him count, remove three, add them again and count again. "Eight," he tells me, "Five and three more is eight. Can I have a snack?"

From 3 PM to 4 PM, I take a break. The children make popcorn and lemonade, and three of them sit around the kitchen table watching a library video about hurricanes and tornados. The middle son spins out of control in the center of the kitchen shrieking, "I am a tornado, I am!!" I grab him and put him in his seat, again, and tell them I am taking "THE" break. I leave the older children's assignment sheets on the table with instructions for the next hour. After the weather video and a snack, the children break out art supplies and begin working on various projects. Jordan sits looking at a book about making paper airplanes, paper and scissors by his side. Skyler sets up her watercolors and begins a new painting, one of a Celtic Moon

Goddess, for history. Her artistic talent is obvious to my trained eye, and these times are encouraged. The younger boys ask to use the computer and sit laughing and learning with Thomas Tank Engine. During this time each day we listen to various CD's for music study; today the children ask for "Classical Kids Mozart's Magic Flute" and listen quietly while they work.

I spend my "break" doing various things: folding laundry, making needed phone calls, and adding a few details to our calendar. I answer questions and stop to lend a hand as I run through the kitchen with laundry and files in my arms. I realize that this is my "break" and finally sit down for 15 minutes to watch the last few minutes of Dr. Phil!

A little after 4 PM, we get ready to leave for ballet class. Skyler has been studying for over six years and is starting to take dance very seriously. I run about the house packing folders and files, wipes, and juice boxes into my tote bag. My daughter runs after me, waist-length hair flying, waving a hairbrush and scrunchi, hoping for the required ballerina bun. The youngest cries; he can't get his shoes on. The middle son screams through the house, up the stairs, down the stairs. He can't find his shoe. The oldest son hangs tightly to the staircase railing, drops his hips to the floor, and begins to scale the wall with his black-soled sneakers. I grab children, assigning direct "to do's". "Help him with his shoes," I yell to Jordan as I remove him from the wall. "Then SIT right THERE until it's time to go." I point at the front steps in the foyer. I run to get my own shoes on and trip over Dakota's lost shoe. After 20 minutes of chaos, we manage to get into the van, the front seat piled with library books, and head to class.

Skyler's class lasts for an hour, so we drop her off and head to the library. The boys spend about 30 minutes picking movies, school videos, and books. As usual, we run into many acquaintances, fellow homeschoolers who remark on the growth of the children and share new curriculum ideas. We recommend a few great books to them and head to checkout with our massive armloads of "finds". I spend the next five minutes removing the middle son from various climbing surfaces while the librarian laughs and discusses the books we chose with the other two boys.

Half an hour later, with all four children in tow, I rush through the grocery store picking up a few needed odds and ends. My oldest son walks down the aisles, hand out, knocking items from the shelf, the youngest yells for a blue "huggie" drink from the cart. The middle son runs from shelves collecting coupons from the automatic dispensers, waving them as though they had value to a five-year-old boy! Six different people stop to remark on the children. "You have your hands full" is the comment most heard, followed by "they are so well behaved and sweet." I smile and pat the middle sons head fondly — if they only knew! "Yes," I say, "and we are homeschoolers." This remark is followed by looks of sheer amazement. I have been called a "saint," and told that I "have the patience of Job." Again, I think, "If they only knew!"

We arrive home shortly after 6 PM, and the children set about sorting library resources. I start a quick dinner, peanut butter and jelly sandwiches, bananas and yogurt, as requested by the youngest. He stands on a kitchen chair beside me, spreading peanut butter onto the bread, telling me a story about apples and hidden stars, acting very much the big boy. As the children eat dinner, I pop onto the computer to pay a few bills, and to check the bank balance. Then I contemplate our schedule for the rest of the week. It looks like a busy one, and I wonder exactly how long a human can go without a private moment.

After cleaning up dinner, the older children play Math War with flashcards while I bathe the younger children. We then set about doing our math program, which is very exhausting for me, the teacher. We use Saxon Math; and while it is wonderful, accelerated, and highly praised by the homeschool community, it is a challenge and chore for me to teach. It is, for the teacher, repetitive and a bit tedious, especially when using it with several small children. Each child sits with me individually, reviewing concepts, learning concepts, using math manipulatives to conjure up correct answers. The other children sit looking at books, working on projects, enjoying a chance for some free reading. My daughter interrupts the lessons; I reprimand her, explaining our rule about "math time" again. This continues until she is sent to work in her room. This outcome is not a happy one, though common. Sometimes there are tears, sometimes there is door slamming, but not today. She grabs her book and heads to her room, I remind her to complete her worksheet and she shoots me a look. I ask if she plans to watch the movie we picked at the library or intends to go to bed early. She smiles coyly and goes up the steps. We finish math without issue and our "school day" is done!

At 7:55 PM, I sit down to get some co-op work done. I pull out my files and calendars, pull our site up on the internet and instant message (IM) a fellow co-op mom, my close friend,

Shelley. We chat briefly, discussing the possibility of an actual LIVE conversation, and end up on the phone. We discuss EVERYTHING, and then finally get down to the business of the co-op. We talk about placing new ads, plan our upcoming field-trip, and the prospect of meeting for a coffee to complete our planning. I pull out my calendar file and begin to go over dates and my availability for the next few weeks. I begin to list our schedule, "ballet, musical theater camp, baseball trophy/pizza party, library workshops, baton camp, soccer practice, church responsibilities..." Shelley laughs and makes a remark about my "under-socialized homeschoolers", a common joke among us. We decide to hang on a few days and try to plan again; my schedule is crazy, and hers is not so great either. We discuss mutual friends, the children, and soon she hangs up to go read her son, Robbie, three-and-a-half, a story. I continue working on the co-op calendar and site until Julian comes looking for some "mommy time".

Julian and I spend the rest of the evening together. He plays cars on the floor while I sort through papers, clean up bookshelves, pick up math manipulatives, and talk with him about his day. At three and a half, he has an amazing vocabulary and a knack for conversation. He tells me about his Snoopy, about the police car from earlier, and, then, that he is not a little boy but a kitty cat. I explain Snoopy's aversion to cats, and he decides he is a dog. He smiles a mischievous grin and remarks, "Skyler is a piggy." I think of her probable reaction to that and laugh. My fourth child is like the pot of gold at the end of the rainbow–a truly beautiful, wonderful star!

Tonight is a lucky night for Julian! He loves the moon, and tonight the moon is out, a tiny crescent in the dark sky across the street from our house. We sit out on our front porch; Julian snuggled in my lap, staring at the moon together. Julian asks to say his "moon prayer" and we begin: "I see the moon, the moon sees me..." The quiet of the night surrounds the two of us, and we sit, silently watching the lightning bugs for quite awhile. This is the best of "mommy time"!

It's 10 PM, and my day is not quite over. I oversee teeth brushing and face washing; find stuffed Snoopys and wandering pillowcases. It's bedtime in our household, and I take that very seriously! I tuck in each child, answering questions about which day of the week "tomorrow" is, what our plans will be, which friends we may see. With a kiss on all four foreheads, I am off—to "my" time!

My husband calls me after the children have been put to bed. We discuss our days; he tells me he won't be home until after 1 AM, and has a chance for overtime this weekend. I tell him a funny story about the kids; he tells me he left his dinner at home. Our conversation is short, his machine is running, and I have an article to work on. I tell him I will be up when he gets home and hang up. It's time to get some work done!

I spend the rest of my evening working on various projects. I work on articles for my website and update some homeschooling plans in my tracking program. This time flies by as I get lost in my writing and soon realize it's well after midnight. I save my work and pop onto my messenger to visit with another close co-op friend for a few minutes before logging off and heading to bed. Many nights end very much the same way my days begin; I throw in a load of laundry and take a few minutes to myself. Fortunately, there is never any door slamming!

Usually I am in bed with a stack of books and notes when my husband comes home from work. Tonight, however, I decide to watch a video I have saved for a treat. I pop some popcorn and climb into bed to relax. I will admit, however, my notebook is by my side—a homeschooling mom's work is never done! When my husband arrives home after 2 AM, I am taking notes for history in the fall. He showers and we eat a snack together, discussing our day. I notice that it's almost 4 AM, and we both shake our heads, laugh, and head up to bed. The door slamming begins in four hours!

First Day of School

Jeannie V, 22, Norway
Dream-filled mother of one

Jeannie, a married mother of one (age 11 months) living in Norway, has gone from "fun-loving club-hopper, Orlando theme-park employee, au pair, wife and mother" in just two short years. She is now about to embark on a recurring role as high school student. "American high school is not enough education to attend college in Norway, so I am attending the last two years of Norwegian high school, so that I can further my education and help provide for my family." A true optimist, Jeannie says, "I am excited to see what happens in the next two years. With some faith, trust, and a little pixie dust, dreams really can come true."

I awake at 7:00 AM. Not really my choice, but my son who has the bed next to me decides every morning when he thinks I should be up. He gets his breastmilk, which definitely hurts me with his new teeth, and we play in bed for a little while. I enjoy every minute with him. But before I get too teary-eyed, I hand him over to his Pappa and check my e-mail. I return to my precious son, Ruben, and gladly give him a diaper change. I let him play on the floor and try to eat some food myself.

It's 8.25 AM, and I am crying. How can I do it? Am I such a horrible mother? Ruben turns a year in almost two weeks. Can I really drop him of at a nanny for the first time? Is going back to school really worth leaving my own son for seven hours five days a week? Ok, I clean up with some comfort from the husband and get ready to go.

At 9:45 AM I leave my son for the longest time in a year. Although this is the first day of school, it is a short day. And he is home with Pappa today. But in my mind, I know what is to come. This is now the beginning of a new year. How will I handle it? Am I going to be water-works all day? ALL YEAR??

In school, I can not help but, well, think of school. I am so concentrated on the business that I need to attend to there. It is only during a break that I think of my son. The breastfeedings, rocking, walking him ALL night to sleep, playing, crying (on both sides) and spitting up all catch up to me. All the hours I spent wanting to get away, to have just five minutes to myself. AND NOW I SHOULD FEAR BEING AWAY!! But I do not. I am balancing the new life. I am a modern mother. I am understanding that what is best for my son is for me to finish my education. This is what is best in our scenario.

The end of the first day of school and my husband comes to pick me up. There is my baby in the passenger seat. (We have an older car without an airbag) Will he be happy to see me? Did he miss me? I can not wait to see his smile when he sees Mamma. Racing to the car door, I look in the window. He is asleep. I stagger into the back seat and stare at him the whole ride home, asking my husband the hows, wheres, and whys of his day. Luckily for me, my son awakes once we are home and leans towards me. He clings for minutes to me before wanting to play again. That cling...that hug, reminds me even more that, although I had to leave him, it is for him...for us that I do it. I may not have been worried at school about him, but, as soon as I saw him, he was my entire life.

I am not a horrible mother. I am just facing the circumstances that have been dealt to me in life. There is no one rule or time-line for life. I am a wife, student, friend...and above all a Mother. This is the one word that embodies so many other words. That gives me hope, inspiration, aspirations and confidence. I am proud to be Jeannie, mother of Ruben.

Graduation Day

Carrie M, 30, South Dakota
Graduating mother of three

Carrie, a married mother of three children (ages 9, 5 and 3) and recent college grad, describes herself as eccentric, confident and down-to-earth. One who revels in the unexpected, she also loves reading, writing, and volunteer work. "A lot of people think since I write humor, that I can take things easily. That said, it is hard to let my guard down and show people that I am a compassionate person with emotional needs."

12:00 AM Of course I am still awake. Even though at 10 PM I wanted to go to bed because I was so tired, I am still awake. My five-year-old son is sleeping soundly next to me on my bed, a bed I can't seem to get him out of even though I have tried my darndest to get him to sleep in his own bed. I know he shouldn't sleep with us, but it is so comforting to see my little man in silent peace, with his go-go-go personality. This sight is a blessing. He is my affectionate child, the one that is constantly hugging and kissing. His feelings get hurt perhaps a bit easier than most, and I wonder how he will react to the conformity of kindergarten this year. His individuality is so unique and his creativeness is shocking in what he perceives and imagines. I hope the school teachers will see the gift of emotions he has and do not try to stifle his visions and uniqueness.

Today I graduate from college and imagine this is why I am still awake. Hemming and hawing over the last-minute details for the big party after the graduation. It also seems that lately I have really been questioning the path I have taken. Why did I go through vie years of college, only to come to the conclusion that the best place for me in this world is home?

Even though I am excited, I also feel a bit letdown. Now what do I do with my life?

7:00 AM I awoke this morning to my youngest daughter next to my side of the bed, a cup in one hand and a carton of orange juice in the other. She wants me to pour her a cup. I kick myself a bit because my children know me well enough to know that I don't like to wake up early, so they help themselves to make it as easy on me as possible.

7:05 AM The juice has been drunk and now we lie holding each other in our arms in the bed. This time is most precious to me because my three-year-old is a running, screaming supremacy child during the day. I often wonder how she became such an ornery child, but then I see what she has to put up with to get my attention, a fact in question when I feel as if I could never possibly find anymore attention to give.

8:50 AM We fell asleep cuddled in each other's arms and now the whole clan is waking up. My oldest girl, who is 9, has already poured herself some cereal and is stationed in front of the television. Once upon a time when I was just beginning the incredible adventure of being a mother, I vowed that I would never let my kids watch too much television. That vow was soon broken.

9:15 AM I am now just starting to iron everyone's clothes for the graduation ceremony today. Feeling way stressed out. How many college graduates really go through the preparations of readying their children and husband before their own graduation? Maybe they were smart by having a family after they went through college, but, to be quite honest, I don't think I would have done as well as I did or be as devoted to my schooling if I didn't have my family at home counting on me.

11:00 AM Everyone is sitting down to a light lunch and I am still running around trying to do five different things and still keep my make-up and sanity intact. I have been so busy that I missed breakfast and lunch, almost an everyday occurrence lately. When I make breakfast and lunch for the kids, I never seem to get that chance to sit down and eat with them. I'm more like the waitress, running and fetching to their needs.

1:00 PM I have to leave for the ceremony before everyone else, to do a quick run-through for seating, etc. It's nice to be alone for the thirty-minute drive. I am excited and nervous about the graduation, and so relieved to be done.

2:15 PM Here I sit with my fellow classmates waiting for our names to be called and to accept our diplomas. I hear a couple of screams from the audience and know instinctively that the sounds are coming from my little one's mouth. I feel relieved that I am not the one dealing with this tantrum right now. My husband is wielding a kicking, screaming child down the corridor and out the door.

My name is called and I hear the hoots and hollers from the audience. My family is very vocal. Good thing they didn't bring the blow horns that they talked about.

2:45 PM It's official. I now have my Bachelor of Science degree, and I graduated with honors. WOOHOO!

3:15 PM The students are now standing outside to get our group photos taken, and I see my husband and my youngest looking for me in the crowd of people. They soon spot me in the group pose, and my daughter is waving frantically at me. I wave to her, and, in her eyes, it is so odd; but, in her three-year-old eyes, I see her eyes full of pride. Right then and there, it all paid off. It was a hard five years, studying, writing, taking classes. It was even more difficult because I had a preschooler when I started and, later, two more newborns while attending college. I used to get so frustrated when I would try to study at home and the house would be rocking with shrieks, squeals and activity. Many times I thought about giving up, giving in to the demands of everyday life as a mother. Now I see why I didn't give up.

5:00 PM It's officially time to party. My son is running around my friend's farm with my graduation cap on, my oldest is performing a wonderful stint, as hostess and my youngest is eating a plateful of cookies for her supper. A band will be coming soon to perform their rocking musical talents for three hours, and my guests are starting to show up.

10:00 PM My two youngest ones went home earlier, all pooped out from the day's events. My oldest is still with us, dancing and having a great time. I am so glad she stayed. She wanted to go home earlier but I coaxed her into staying. Lately our relationship has been a bit strained. I forget what it is like to be a nine-year-old. The growing process is beginning for her and I think we are both a bit uncomfortable with this transition. I want her to be so much, and I think I expect a great deal out of her, probably too much. My patience with her, while she learns new attitudes and perceptions, has been so thin lately. She has always been my experiment in rearing children and I can't seem to shake the feeling that I have failed. Yet I know she is a loving creature. I just wish I could start over with her and do things differently. I would have shown her my love instead of telling her and expecting her to know that I love her.

But back to the here and now; she is dancing the night away and having a blast. I do so love her. I'll go show her.

11:00 PM The night is coming to a close but the party is showing no signs of stopping. The day was wonderful, my friends and family there to help make my day great. They have made my life what it is now.

First Full Day of Summer: How Long Can 24 Hours Feel?

Kelley C, 40, New Jersey
"Surviving the day" mom of three

Kelley Cunningham Cousineau, a former advertising art director, is now a married mother at home with her three boys (ages 10, 8 and 5-1/2). "I reject the notion that once we have children we become marginalized and categorized in our society. Our womanliness, sexiness, intelligence, other interests, etc. must be sacrificed if we are to be seen as 'good mother.' Every mother must find her own way, and I've finally found mine through humor, art, poetry, and writing."

6:30 AM My husband rumbles to life but I lie in bed half-awake, vaguely aware that this morning feels different. I don't have the mental capacity at this caffeine-challenged hour to fathom what the reason could possibly be. So be it, I'm going back to sleep. This is heaven! I should be able to snooze for another half-hour. Or at least until the children park themselves next to my bed holding out their cereal bowls.

6:32 AM My five-year-old crawls in for a cuddle. So much for my nap. Yes, he's darling, but can't he wait till seven o'clock to exhibit all his charms?

6:45 AM A few prods in the chops from bony little elbows force me to abandon my tribute to sloth. I should get going. Lunches to make. Are there any cheesefood slices left? I have to remember to scour out that lunchbox so the drosophila stop propagating in it. Oh shit, I'm out of juice boxes. And all the water bottles leak.

6:47 AM Hey, wait! Today is the first day of summer vacation! I don't have to make any lunches! No schlepping for me today!

6:48 AM But what am I going to do with them all day? Strange, even though yesterday was the last day of school, I was in denial. I could sort of forget that I had two and a half months of 24/7 Quality Time ahead of me to endure.

7:00 AM "Can we play video games?"

7:15 AM "We're hungry!"

7:45 AM "Mom, can you get up and come downstairs? Skippy spilled the orange juice!"

7:45 AM I wipe up the orange juice and clean up the breakfast mess. I don't know what's worse, making their breakfast or letting them do it and cleaning up afterwards. I make my coffee and slump over the paper with my caffeine drip and tell them to leave me alone.

8:30 AM Ah, that's better. I'm alive now. Hmm, wonder where the kids are?

8:40 AM I finally find them playing video games. I make the usual lame threat to throw the "Goddamn Game Cube" out the window, but they know I'm just whistling in the wind. They know I need it for free babysitting like a junkie needs a fix. They yawn and shuffle dejectedly out of the room. "Go outside and play!" "It's raining." "Well, go find something to do."

8:45 AM "Mom, can we make a cyclone experiment? We saw it on Zoom." Damn. I can't think of a good reason to say no and they sense my weakness, like hyenas surrounding a lame antelope. I fish two two-liter bottles out of the recycling, unearth some electric tape from the mountain of crap on my husband's workbench, and find a bottle of food coloring after emptying out my spice cabinet. We build the contraption but despite, my best efforts, it leaks blue water all over the place. The kids give up and go back to visiting Mario and Luigi, while I scour the blue food coloring drops out of the countertop. Damn you, Zoom! Damn you, Durkee Food Coloring!

9:00 AM Now what?

9:01 AM I decide we need a schedule. This lollygagging about is not good for the children. How will they ever adjust to being back in school come September after running wild all summer like so many feral cats? I jump on the computer and make up a Chore Chart and an allowance payment schedule. When I show it to the kids, they are surprisingly receptive. They make their beds, unload the dishwasher and take out the garbage, eager to make check marks on the chart. I stand there disbelieving and watch them with my head cocked to the side like a dog who hears a funny noise.

10:00 AM "We're hungry!

"You may have an apple or a banana."

"Why can't we have gummy bears?"

"Because *Child* magazine said that if I stock up on healthy treats you would gleefully lunge for them. Didn't you kids read the article?"

10:30 AM I pile everyone into the car to go sign up for the Summer Reading Program at the library. I don't know what I've done wrong, but my kids hate books. I've done everything the experts said to do. I read to them till I began shouting, "Do you like my hat? Yes, I like that party hat!" to stunned passers-by. The children see me reading constantly, everything from the Times to People to Camus. That's called modeling proper behavior, right, T. Berry? But when I mention that we're going to the library, they react like I'm asking them to watch paint dry.

"It's BOR-ing."

"How can it be boring? There's a wonderland of imagination waiting for you!"

They roll their eyes and get in the car.

"We're going and you'll learn to like reading if I have to break every bone in your bodies."

10:45 AM There are gaggles of children happily reading,

tra-la, nestled in every nook and cranny of the children's room. "Look, Mommy, a new book by Jamie Lee Curtis! Let's read it together, then dance around the maypole and toss rose petals about!" What the hell? My kids shuffle in as if they're facing the executioner. I try to get them enthused.

"Look at the prizes you can win!"

Then I take a closer look at the prizes. I must admit they're pretty lame. Four hours of reading and all you get is a paper animal to color? Sixteen hours for a bouncy ball? Whoop dee doo. But I hide my disappointment. "Look at what you get for 150 hours!!! A yo-yo!"

They sulk. That's what is wrong with kids nowadays. They don't know how to yoyo.

NOON I decide to take them out to lunch at the diner in town. I walk out twenty-five dollars poorer. Note to self: Suck it up and make more PB & J's at home or else you're going to have to get a real job.

1:15 PM Seeing that I blew big bucks at lunch, I figure I'll get out the clippers and give them their summer buzzcuts. That's fifty bucks I'll save by not going to the barber. Think what that'll buy at Target! And the human hair flying around the backyard will keep the deer out of my neighbor's garden. He should thank me.

2:00 PM Desperate, I call a few of their friends over for playdates. They all promptly disappear in front of the

"Goddamn Game Cube" again. I shoo them outside. I check on them a few minutes later. One boy is hitting a tree with a baseball bat. The other is hitting the sandbox top with a golf club. Another is kicking woodchips from the flowerbed onto the lawn. The rest are taking turns yawning.

"Hey kids! How about some tag or something?"

"That's boring."

2:45 PM "Mom, can you set up the Slip and Slide?" Normally taking on a project like this would be only slightly more palatable than getting a complete Brazilian wax, but today I'm out of better ideas.

3:15 PM Blue-lipped and dizzy from blowing up the damn thing, I stumble over to the hose to turn it on. Thank God it works. I run upstairs to look for bathing suits. Now, where did I put them for the winter? Ah, yes, under the bed. A bit dusty, so what? They'll get clean in the water. Then I hear the tell-tale crinkling of dried-out, useless waistband elastic. The kids wind up mooning the whole neighborhood with every pass down the slip and slide. I wonder what the new mom across the street must be thinking as she watches the two or three hundred boys hurtling themselves across my lawn as I sit slumped in my white resin lawn chair drinking a Bud Lite.

5:00 PM The playdates go home. I decide to go to the town pool to pick up our pool badges, the keys to a summer chockfull of Marco Polo and athlete's foot. Waiting in line with other scantily-clad people in bathing suits, I decide I'm seeing way too much of my neighbors.

6:00 PM Dinnertime. Hmm, what to make? Large pie, half pepperoni, deliver it please. I'll throw them some grapes to ease the guilt and to cut the grease.

7:00 PM "Can we play video games?"

8:00 PM Time for bed. "Hop to it, troops!" You're tired, I can tell.

9:30 PM I said, "Go to bed! I told you that you were tired! Now get to bed. Please?"

9:32 PM My husband comes home after working a late night. He asks what I did all day. "Nothing," I say. I don't have the mental energy to go into the myriad details; and, even if I did, his eyes would glaze over as he feigned interest. He goes upstairs to kiss the children goodnight and gets them all amped up again in the process. It goes from All Quiet on the Western Front to The Good, The Bad and the Ugly within seconds. I don't intervene. He started it so he can deal with it. After a few more minutes, I hear him raise his voice. "Settle Down!" He comes back downstairs and slumps onto the sofa next to me. "Wow, they're a handful!" No shit.

10:00 PM Ah, alone time. They're finally asleep. I curl up with a good book and reflect. After a day like this, even the editors of Family Fun magazine would throw up their hands in defeat and start counting the minutes till school starts again. But I'll get through the summer okay if I can just get this little respite at night to read and think about something other than children.

10:02 PM   Asleep on couch.

Same Stuff, Different Day

"Half this game is 90% mental."
~Yogi Berra

"God grant me the serenity
to accept the things I cannot change;
courage to change the things I can;
and wisdom to know the difference."

~ Leslie C, 28, Canada
Spiritual mom of three (ages 4, 3, and 6 months)

Sometimes I look around the chaos of my life and wondered "When did this happen?" I guess I knew I was in trouble when my OB/GYN, Dr. Christie, handed me my brand new baby boy AND I was still pregnant with another baby! Ha-ha—I knew I was pregnant with twins, but boy, oh boy (literally) life has never been the same! I will say, though, that being a mom has taught me to be humble and gracious in ways that no other experience in my life had.

~ Kathy G, 38, Southern California
Funny mom of three (ages 4 and twins, 10 months)

~

7:05 AM: Rise and shine. I pull on the latest in stay-at-home apparel—the terry cloth sweatsuit and matching jacket with t-shirt—out of the dryer. Attempt to style my hair, but end up pulling it back into a ponytail as I do each day. Time for the day to begin!

~ Jennifer M, 29, Colorado
Stay-at-home mom of one (age 3)

~

Dear Diary,

It's Thursday. It's seems a lot like Wednesday which seems a lot like Tuesday which is a lot like Monday. Anyway, I think you get the picture. My days are a constant whirlwind of dishes, laundry, diapers, boo-boos, Sesame Street, Candy Land and Dora the Explorer. I wouldn't change it for anything.

~ Vickie R, 33, Connecticut
Married mom of two (ages 4 and 2)

~

I'm eating my low-carb lunch of ham and cheese at the computer. Why can't someone create a high-carb diet that would allow me to eat cookies and pasta lunch? Oooh, twenty-five new e-mails. Unfortunately, only five of them are legitimate. The rest are either sale ads or spam. There are also a few porn emails too. I never can figure those out. Sure, I admit, we downloaded the Paris Hilton sex tape once, but that was about all the porn that has hit our computer. Why am I always receiving emails about Viagra and hot moms? I delete them fast. Thank goodness my kids aren't old enough to read.

~ Julie S, 33, Southern California
Dieting mom of 3 (ages 4, 3 and 1)

I have been trying to record a day in the life of raising twins for four months now. I have yet to do it. There is a reason for that; it's crazy and hectic. Although, while it is crazy and hectic, it is also calm and slow—all at the same time. It's hard to explain, but I am sure some of you out there understand that. All I can say is that every single day I get up, go to the nursery, and peek into the crib, and see two beautiful, healthy, happy baby girls; I pinch myself. I never knew having babies would change my life so drastically, and I could never have imagined the kind of love that I have for them. My days are filled with lots of laundry, diapers galore, goo goo and ga ga, spit up, smiles, and a little crying, but mostly PURE JOY.

~ Sara O, 27, Southern California
New mom of two (twins, age 4 months)

...I came across this quote by Don Marquis, "The most pleasant and useful persons are those who leave some of the problems of the universe for God to worry about." I think this is an appropriate quote for today.

~ Tara P, 30, Virginia
Busy mom of two (ages 7 and 3)

So, my son asked a weird question today. He saw a boy in gym class that is uncircumcised. He wants to know why they are different. I'm not really sure what to say. It's times like these that I wish my husband were around. Although, I'm not so sure he'd give him a politically correct answer. I was thinking I could explain it as a face lift. On one penis the skin is pulled rather tight, and on the other the skin is loose. But I'm not sure that's the right way to explain it either. Sure would be helpful if I had a penis instead of a vagina right now.

~ Sara B, 38, Northern California
Gender-quizzing mom of two (ages 13 and 8)

12:01 PM I sometimes wonder if my children were placed here just to drive me absolutely crazy. It is only noon, and I'm done for the day. My son has taken to making up words, so I can't understand him at all. Why can't he just talk normal like other kids? My daughter yells....a lot. I pray for the day when she can just ask me something in a softer volume. At least right now, they are quiet because they are eating peanut butter and banana sandwiches. The peanut butter makes it hard to talk.

~ Jessica M, 25, New Jersey
"Going crazy" mom of two (twins, age 5)

My life is filled with Pampers, playdates and my little "peanuts." I couldn't be happier!

~ Emily W, 26, Oregon
Happy mom of two (ages 2-1/2 and 6 months)

God sure knew what he was doing when he created the serenity prayer, because Lord knows I say it quite frequently with my three boys.

~ Margaret O, 46, Florida
Serenity-seeking mom of three (ages 15, 14, and 12)

My husband and I got a babysitter for this Saturday. Yippee!! We haven't been out on a date for over six months. I can't wait!

~ Claudia O, 34, Iowa
Ecstatic mom of two (ages 7 and 5)

I love mommyhood! I love the coos, the playing, the ruckus. I even love the crying (usually). Yep, maybe I'm weird, but I love every aspect of mommyhood!

~ Jennifer E, 28, North Carolina
Joyous mom of one (age 10 months)

I had a dentist appointment today, and the dentist asked me if I experience a lot of headaches. I laughed and said, "Uh, yeah. I have three kids under five."

~ Terry W, 44, Colorado
Pained mother three (ages 4-1/2 and twins, 3)

Today I realized that I had achieved "complete" motherhood when I heard my children repeating things that I had told them which were things that my mother told me when I was younger. I guess the never-ending cycle of life is true.

~ Linda D, 39, Missouri
Complete mom of three (ages 16, 8, and 7)

Whirlwind Days

Deborah M, 48, Illinois
Hectic-paced mom of five

On her 25th wedding anniversary, Deborah, 48, a married mom of now five children (ages 22, 20, 15, 11 and 6) decided she wanted to make a difference in the world by helping a child in need. "My husband and I have enjoyed parenting our three sons and thought we would add one more boy to our family ~ a boy who needed a family to love him." Soon after, she and her husband started their "journey of faith" to add another son to their family. They were quite surprised when they found that the little boy they were adopting had a sister he'd never met. Deborah and her family committed to raising both children. "It is amazing the path that God weaves for us! Two children at the other end of the world, completely alone, are now a part of our family." Deborah raises awareness on orphanages and international adoption through her various speaking engagements. To find out more about Deborah and her adoption journey, visit www.picturetrail.com/dmumm5.

It's 6:30 AM on Friday, and I get up to take a quick shower before the morning routine begins. I put on nice slacks and a sweater since I have a breakfast meeting with the local Chamber of Commerce at 8:00 AM. I hear Travis, our 20-year-old, leaving the house on his way to his job as a carpenter's apprentice. I wake up Kellen, a freshman in high school, and his sister,

Tania, a fourth grader. I can see Alex, 6, stirring on his bed down the hall. He has pre-school on Wednesday and Friday mornings, so I can work or attend meetings. I head downstairs where our dog, a little Bischon, is anxiously waiting for his breakfast. I feed him and begin making school lunches. The dog barks. Tania cannot get her hair to look right. I sigh. I am not used to the dramatic problems girls have in the morning. Until seven months ago, I was the mom of only three sons, the youngest at that time being 14-years-old. Our lives changed when we decided to adopt one more boy (we felt we were good at raising boys.) We chose to adopt from Russia which has thousands of orphans, mostly boys. On our first trip over to meet Alex we learned he had an older sister in another local orphanage. They had never met each other. After much prayer and consideration, we chose to take Alex's sister, Tania, as well. They are truly wonderful children, and we are very blessed to have them in our family.

On with my day! Kellen and Tania eat their breakfast while a tired Alex appears on the scene. He resists getting dressed as he'd rather stay home than go to pre-school. Alex is very small in size and has had many changes in his life this year. We have decided to hold him back a year to have his language and social skills catch up so he can do kindergarten next year. In between coaching him to dress and eat, I put on my make up. Kellen's ride appears at 7:30 AM; he grabs his things and leaves. Tania can't find her gloves, and I do a mad search for them. She grabs her bag and gives me a kiss good-bye at 7:35 AM as she heads down the street to catch the school bus. My husband, Dennis, appears in the kitchen ready for work. He takes over with Alex, so I can get to my breakfast meeting. Alex gives me a big hug and kiss, and I'm off to my meeting.

After an hour or so of networking, breakfast and business exchanges, I am in the van heading back home.

I am happy to have a home-based business where I can set my own hours for work. However, I have found with the two newest children here I don't have a lot of hours to do work anymore. Now that they speak English, things have settled down somewhat, so that helps. I make a few phone calls, return emails, and try to "find" my desk in my office. Soon it is 11:45 AM and time to pick up Alex from pre-school.

Thirty minutes later, we are home. We get his school bag ready for the Pre-K program he attends during the afternoon. Wednesday and Friday are the hardest since he has back-to-back school, but he is thriving in these programs and is very happy! He does resist the "leaving home process," and we usually have to bribe him with taking the dog out on the leash to wait for the bus to come. He likes that. The bus comes at 12:45 PM, and he happily jumps on board. I head back to my office for a little more work.

I grab a bite to eat and then try to get some work done at my desk. I am working on some online training to improve my website and business. I never seem to have the time to get too far on them. Our oldest son, Brandon, is away at college; I send him a quick email. I also try to take advantage of my brief alone time to run to the store for those few groceries we always seem to need. I clean up the breakfast and lunch dishes before Tania comes home at 3:00 PM. We get a chance to talk about her day and look at her papers. Kellen calls at 3:30 PM for a ride from the bus stop, which is about five blocks away. I get him in the door, and he is immediately in the refrigerator looking for food. I cut some fruits and veggies, which my two newest kids still feel is a great snack, and get ready for Alex's bus to appear. Alex bounds into the door with his coat and shoes thrown off immediately. He and Kellen wrestle for a few minutes before they take a break to eat.

The doorbell rings and two of Tania's girlfriends appear. Alex loves having people over too, so he is immediately running around and showing off. The dog barks at all the excitement. To think, a year ago I thought our home was starting to get a bit too quiet!

My office phone rings, and it is a customer with a question. I try to hide in my office where maybe it might be quieter. Usually Alex comes in and asks question of me when I do this. He hasn't learned the difference of my office phone and family phone yet, as far as interruptions go.

From 4:00 PM to 6:00 PM, Tania and Alex beg for food. After living in an orphanage, they are still not used to having so much food around. They never saw food prepared before living here. Food always just appeared on the table at supper time. There was never second helpings. So, they love having so much to choose from now. It takes great patience to cook with them around as they are always trying to take food off the counters. I try to not let them have much, so they will eat supper with us later.

Travis appears around 5:00 PM from work and heads for the shower after playing with Alex for a few minutes. The dog again is impatient for food and begins barking and running in circles by the refrigerator. I can't stand all the noise, so I feed him. I throw in another load of laundry. I have to do two to three loads a day just to maintain control.

Tania's friends decide to leave after playing several games, all which involved lots of screaming and giggling. Tania and Alex watch TV for a few minutes of peace and quiet.

Dennis appears home from work, and we try to sit down at the table for supper. It is not a quiet supper as everyone always seems to have things to say, usually all at the same time. After preparing supper for 45 minutes, it is rather discouraging that it only takes about five to seven minutes for everyone to eat and be done. The kids bring dishes to the sink, and I finish scraping and loading them into the dishwasher.

We play some games with Kellen, Tania and Alex. Now it's time for the bedtime routines. Alex gets into the tub about 7:30 PM. After playing, reading a story, brushing teeth, and kissing everyone good night, he is in bed for the night. Tania, having been in the orphanage as well as having bad past life experiences, still requires me to be in the bathroom with her while she showers. With her being a girl, this sometimes takes an hour or more of my time. We play a game of cards with her before she heads to bed at 9:30 PM. Kellen plays his X-Box Live in his room while Travis spends time on the computer or phone with his girlfriend. Dennis watches TV. I usually join him by 10:00 PM. I watch the news, but I am so tired I have trouble staying awake much past 11:00 PM or so.

I plop into bed exhausted. For the most part, it is a good

exhaustion. I have five great kids, a home-based business I enjoy, and a supportive husband. Friday nights are my favorite, though, as I know I don't have to wake-up to an alarm clock the next day. However, I'm sure Alex will get me up before 8:00 AM, and yet another hectic day will begin.

Rush, Rush, Rush

Shawna A, 48, Southern California
Busy, busy, busy mother of three

Shawna is the mother of three children (ages 15, 13 and 3) is passionate about her family, which leaves little time for her hobbies. However, she does try to work in time for her favorite pastimes which are psychic readings, gardening, and time with her spouse. "Put your relationship with your husband first. A happy marriage is the most important gift you can give your children."

6:25 AM A quickie shower.

6:30 AM Breakfast with Jenna, my 13-year-old. She does her own hair. So cute, but she always wants my opinion. I'm grateful she still cares what I think. I check her make-up. Looks pretty. Not too dark.

6:45 AM Jenna's out the door. Makes the bus! Casey, my 15-year-old son, shows up for breakfast and we hang out while he eats. I do some dishes and make some lunches.

7:30 AM My husband, Pete, and Casey leave for work and school. Mike, my three-year-old son, wants breakfast and to watch a super hero movie. Antibiotics for Mike and the dog, as well. I finish drying my hair and comb Mike's. Fold a load of clothes. Do dishes. Water my flower pots out front. Walk Snowflake, our dog.

8:30 AM Drop Mike at preschool. Kiss-kiss. Have fun. Three free hours for mom. Yes!

9:00 AM Jenna's cookie order is dropped off with her cheer coach. Casey's tux is returned in the other direction. I register Mike for swim lessons. Catch up with two girlfriends on my cell during my errands: drycleaning, Sav-On for prescription. Home for two minutes to move laundry and put in a pan of cookies for later.

11:30 AM Pick up Mike.

NOON Podiatrist appointment. Very painful injection during which my adorable three-year-old lay on my tummy and smothered me with kisses, so it wouldn't hurt.

12:30 PM At McDonalds where the same, not so adorable, child cried and kicked for 15 minutes, because we drove through McD's and didn't have time to go in and play.

1:00 PM Home. Arrive at the same time as (1) Culligan Man for repairs, (2) another repair man for demolition and repair of leaking shower (yikes!), (3) a friend and her son, whom I'm watching today, and (4) another friend and her two boys. The phone rings non-stop and the repair men have questions. Why did I think I could just visit friends while they were here?

2:00 PM Finally the phone stops and workmen are gone. June and I watch our boys swim and play on Slip & Slide. We talk diets, exercise, how cute our kids are, and about her new dress.

2:45 PM June leaves. Her boys stay. I call my sweetie and talk a bit. I eat way more chocolate chip cookies than I should (these are the ones I baked earlier for "the kids.") Jenna arrives home with a friend who is locked out of her house. Four boys between the ages of three to five and two 13-year-old girls: It's loud in here right now! My 15-year-old calls. Can he stay at school to watch a ball game? Sure. I serve ice cream, kiss a couple boo-boos, and put out a tiff. Move laundry. Move around picking up the house.

3:45 PM All four boys leave. Jenna's friend is no longer locked out, and she goes home. Casey is home from school. I am picking up Legos—lots and lots and lots of Legos. There is something calming, almost meditative about the repetition of picking up and delivering handfuls of Legos. Being upstairs alone and having a quiet house helps, although, the entire time, I hear a fire truck dinging sound in the distance—like a car alarm or a truck backing up. It turns out to be an emergency vehicle right in the room, but subdued to very weak batteries. No doubt it's been alarming for most of the day.

4:00 PM I sit down to do a psychic reading. Often times, "work" is the easiest part of my day. Casey and Jenna watch Mike for me.

5:30 p. m. Starting dinner. Big kids are emptying the dishwasher, folding laundry, helping with Mike. Yes, I know I'm lucky. I also know that I will refold 50 percent of the laundry after my son goes to bed. As I patiently coach him on his laundry style, the percentage of refolding has been going down. I walk the dog—a perfect kid-chore, but I enjoy the walk, so I assign it to me and my three-year-old even though I'm still limping on the foot that saw the podiatrist earlier.

6:30 PM Pete's home and helps with math homework. Mike gets a Wheat Thin cracker stuck in his throat and throws up. He recovers after some loving.

6:45 PM Dinner outside. It's a very warm and pretty night. Joke around with the older kids about whom they'd like to go out with. We play a game of "keep away" with a winged football that's hung out in the sun way too long. Fun and giggles.

8:00 PM I take a bath with Mike, snuggle in bed with him, and read two books (after he routinely rejects the first half-dozen that I suggest). Dad and I take our time tucking in the kids, and, yes, we still tuck in the 13- and 15-year-old with kisses and wishes for sweet dreams, share some backrubs, and highlights of the day. It takes longer than it should, but we do it anyway. I offered to help Pete with a project we are working on. He was almost finished and did not need me. I'm grateful.

9:40 PM We've never seen *Sex and the City* and just bought the first season. We decide to watch an episode together and just unwind. NOTE TO SELF: *Sex and the City* is not a wind-down kind of program.

A Grand Mother

Michelle A, 62, Florida
Mother of two and grandmother of one

Michelle, a mother of two (ages 38 and 35) and grandmother of one (age 2), transplanted herself from Boston to Florida to live near her family. A giving woman dedicated to the well-being of her family, Michelle is a primary care-giver in her granddaughter's life. "My daughter has frequent hospital stays, so I take Briana, my two-almost-three-going-on-thirty-year-old for two days a week. This allows my daughter a much needed break from this little, active, talkative toddler—who is also very bright and beautiful, mind you." Striving for business success and personal satisfaction, Michelle formed her own at-home art designing personalized pictures for children. To find out more about Michelle, log onto www.michellescreations.net.

I pick up my granddaughter, Briana, from pre-school every Wednesday. When she sees me today, she shouts, "This is my "Nah Nah!" I swear she can be heard in Boston. She has a very loud voice. I wonder if she might be an opera singer as she loves music, and her scream can break a glass. We finally make our way to my car, which she has decided is old, like me. She says that she will buy me a new, red card someday. I live in a rural area that is just north of Tampa. We check all the local cows and horses. Briana is fascinated with the American Flag, and we count them. Last week I bought her two small flags.

Briana is my miracle baby. Her mother has severe endometriosis and a very serious ulcerative colitis condition. Doctors told my daughter that she would never be able to have a baby. She had a very painful cyst that needed medical treatment. When they did an ultrasound on the cyst, they also found a little miracle. Two weeks later they determined that the baby was a girl. (I'm crying as I type this.) My daughter has no colon, as it was so diseased that it had to be removed. She also developed a chronic sinus condition. I've done research and think it is from a fungal allergy. Unfortunately, doctors are unable to find the bacteria causing the infection.

When we arrive home, Briana immediately sets herself up on my sofa bed, which she refers to as her "sofa bed couch." She removes her shoes and socks and makes herself at home with an array of assorted blankets, and, of course, her dearly beloved Elmo which mommy packs in her overnight suitcase.

I offer Briana some food. Some of the food her mommy sends and some of it is food that I know Briana enjoys. She has a tiny appetite and will only eat a little. There are some days when we stop at McDonald's. We don't tell mommy, because she disapproves of fast food. We aren't making those stops anymore, though, because Briana will only eat two fries and two chicken nuggets. It isn't worth the expense. She really just wants the toy, anyway.

We spend the day watching and discussing videos. Presently, she adores Babar the Elephant. I tell her that I think that Elmo is jealous since she used to watch him exclusively. She enjoys animal stories, numbers and the alphabet. She sings the alphabet song and can recognize most letters and ever some words. She colors, uses crayons, pencils, and markers. She loves to use stickers and has created some glorious artwork on my refrigerator and walls. We read stories, play, and tickle each other. She is the love of my life.

Dinner is a hassle with Briana. She is so fussy. Then it's off to bath. Most of the time, I take a shower with her and all the rubber duckies, frogs, and other toys covering my bathroom. I always think about the first time I undressed in front of her. She looked at me and said, "Milk." (Yes, she remembered those infant days with mommy.) She tried to compare our breast size pointing to hers and saying, "Small." I stopped her before she described mine.

Going to bed is difficult; Briana would stay up all night if she could. After several stories, putting her back to bed, hiding, and even pretending that I am sleeping, it is finally quiet. I watch the "Super Nanny" on television to get some bedtime tips. I awake in the morning with the cutest little toddler sleeping next to me. I heard her come in quietly during the night with all her blankets, Elmo, and whatever else she can fit in her two hands.

So how do I feel about this little, active toddler? I light up when I see her. She is my very, special little girl. I love her so much. I hate to admit this, but I do not remember having such strong feelings for my two children. There is something special between a "nah nah" and her grandchild. I am exhausted when she is here, but as soon as she goes home, I miss her. It is a good feeling to be a grandparent. I feel young again.

Loving the Chaos

Kelly E, 36, Wisconsin
Optimistic mother of three

Kelly, a married mother of three (ages 4-1/2 and twins, 2-1/2), living in Wisconsin, is proud to be a strong woman with a natural instinct to nurture. An admitted people pleaser, she still know that "me" time is essential to her well-being. "No matter what obstacles are in my way or how bad or stressful our day-to-day life gets, I always give 100 percent of myself to my family. My kids, husband, family and friends have molded me into the woman I am today!"

Ok, it's 10 PM and it's quiet. Hard to believe all three of my kiddos are sleeping. So my handsome husband, Steve, and I have time for each other!! Yippee!!! Ehhhhhhhh! Wrong answer. He has to work. Steve works full time but has a growing side business. He has an office set up in our recreation room. Well, at least I can look at him and have minimal conversation as my desk and computer are right across from him!!

As I sit here zoning (knowing that I should be in bed right now), I am counting the zits on my face. I am very attractive but you can't notice that because of the giant mounds on my face. I feel very ugly! I've started naming my blemishes. That's pretty sad, I know. I can't believe I'm saying this, but I can't wait for my yearly visit to the OB/GYN. I want her to prescribe something to regulate my hormones. Hopefully, that will help my skin. Lord knows I've tried everything. Well, I haven't tried moving away from my family and all the stressors in my life, and I won't do that ever!! Time for mommy to go to sleep—or at least to try. I'm praying it's an uneventful evening!!!

It's 6 AM, and time to start the day. I finally got sleep. Not comfortable, energizing sleep, but sleep nonetheless. Just got back from taking Nash, our six-month-old Silver Labrador, for his morning walk. It's more like he was walking me. We're back, and Nash gets to eat. That means mommy gets her first sip of coffee in peace! Wait, I take that back. Our two-and-a-half-year-old son, Alexander, has just awoken whimpering. I tried straightening his blankets and sneaking out, but to no avail. He's screaming at this point and has awakened his twin brother, Austin, and his big sister Jenna. Yay, me! Steve just got out of the shower and hears all the commotion. I know he wants to turn around and jump back in the shower! He helps change Alexander and Austin's diapers and puts them back to bed. My back has been aching for days now, and I think I aggravated it again lifting Alexander out of bed. He's not light. He's about 33 lbs and growing! Not chunky, just a big, solid boy. I'm in pain with my back, and I begin to cry. I'm basically in the fetal position, and my daughter Jenna, who is four-and-a-half, tries to comfort me by rubbing my back. Steve tries to work the knot out and gets me two ibuprofen.

Ok, a bit of normalcy has returned. Jenna needs breakfast. I need a shower. Today is Alexander and Austin's therapy playgroup. Every Monday and Wednesday from 9 AM to 11 AM they have a combined group of therapists and other kids with special needs. My sweet boys were born three months early. We made it to 28 weeks gestation. They also had Twin-to-Twin Transfusion Syndrome in utero. It's a disease of the placenta. Our boys received unequal shares of nutrition through the blood vessels. Alexander received 80 percent and Austin received 20 percent. My boys are true miracles of God.

Alexander and Austin are developmentally delayed in most areas. That is why they had been receiving in-home therapy three to four times per week since they came home from the hospital in 2002. We've now advanced to the therapy playgroup at the rehabilitation center. The boys are doing great. They receive physical, occupational, speech, and special education services. It's a very nice program and we are thankful our boys were able to get in. There is limited space.

I'm out of the shower, and I start getting Jenna dressed. She's all set. The boys wake up and it's time to start the assembly line of feeding, changing diapers, getting the boys dressed, getting everyone out the door on time. I have a feeling I will be late again! It's 8:10 AM already, and we need to leave by 8:30-ish AM!

We're in the mini-van and I decide to call Steve at work to let him know that the toilet in our second bathroom does not work-it won't flush. This happened five minutes before we left for therapy. Geez, I love Mondays. He's not mad. Just another task to do when he gets home.

It's 10 AM; therapy has been going for an hour already. Jenna and I are in the family room waiting for Alexander and Austin's session to be over. I stand by the door, just enough to see out, and hoping the boys do not see me. Both of them are getting assistance walking down the hallway. Austin is pushing a cart for balance and Alex has his hand held by one of the therapists. Neither boy walks on his own yet. It's one moment at a time for Alex and Austin. We take each accomplishment they do and celebrate it. As the boys walk by our doorway—and still don't see us—a smile appears on my face. It's amazing to see how far they have come since the day of their birth two-and-a-half years ago. They came into this world at a combined weight of four pounds and 11-1/2 ounces!

As I watch them walk by, my smile turns to tears. I watch Alexander and Austin struggle to do the simple things we take for granted: holding an object, walking, talking, etc. I see Austin, my little "midgey," struggle with everything. He doesn't seem to be moving forward with his daily activities as his brother Alex. There is an underlying chance Austin might be mildly mentally retarded (MMR). It's a diagnosis our family was told about last September when our boys were evaluated by a voluntary program. It's a diagnosis my husband and I chose "not" to deal with or dwell upon until necessary. We're giving both of our boys every resource and opportunity in all programs available to them. But, lately and silently, I have been carrying this heavy load on my shoulders. I have a gut feeling that my little "midgey" is MMR. I am ready to deal with it. Steve has not focused on it. We love Austin and Alexander unconditionally no matter what challenges they face. We will get them through all obstacles. My boys are so special to me. You have no idea how much love is in my heart for my two miracles.

Its 12:30 PM, I just put Alexander and Austin down for a nap. Now Jenna and I can have some time together. I've decided to wash our minivan. Jenna gets completely soaked and thinks she is helping me by putting her wet cloth through the mud and then back on to the van! Hey, the van is clean. Good job! We decide to eat lunch!! I have a salad. I need to get rid of the six pounds I gained since May. I lost 23 pounds (yes, I pat myself on my back) in the past 11 months. I look good again!

Jenna has a sandwich and wants to watch another Disney movie, which is fine by me. I need some silent time. I get a bottle of water and scan the junkyard (otherwise known as my house). I'm not worrying about dishes, wash, and whatever else is out of its place any more. There are so many other things to worry about and deal with every day.

It's around 3 PM. I had to make several important phone calls. Also, I need to get dinner ready. Something easy tonight. A neighbor girl is over playing with my daughter Jenna. They are playing nicely, which is surprising. Alexander and Austin are finally up from their nap. I give the kids a snack and some juice to tide them over until dinner. They are playing on the floor and staring at the television, which is shut off. I know they are waiting for a video. So what shall it be—Elmo, Nemo, or Blue's Clues? Elmo's the winner! I'm not a big fan of sticking my kids in front of the TV, but the smiles on their faces when they watch their favorite video is priceless for me.

Steve just got home. It's around 4:30 PM, otherwise known as the "witching hours" at our house. Everyone is antsy from a long day and very little patience is seen. Tonight the boys will eat separately from us. With the busy day, I did not have time to make a special dinner for the boys. Due to Austin's severe peanut and egg allergies, there are lots of food items he cannot eat. The dinner we are having tonight is has some of those foods he cannot eat. So I whip up mashed potatoes, veggies, and a beef hot dog for the twins. Yum, yum, I know. But it's filling, and they like it.

Dinner is ready for us. I serve everyone first, as always. Then I get to sit down and eat. As usual, the princess, a.k.a. Jenna, summons me as if I am a waitress at the local diner. "Mom, where's my milk? I can't eat this breadstick, it's broken." And so on! As much as she frustrates me, I love the independent and strong willed little lady she is turning out to be. She's a handful, believe me, but that's our Jenna. She's amazingly smart. I always say she's four-and-a-half going on 14! Jenna is very advanced in all levels for her age. She's a beautiful little girl, so full of energy—wish I could get me some of that!! Not only am I her mother, but also we're friends. That is important to both of us.

It's now 7:00 PM. The evening got away from us once again. We did not get to go for that walk after dinner. I'm still having back spasms from this morning. So we're off to Toyland—our living room. All three kids are running amuck, and the dog is chasing all three of them. Steve and I just sort of look at each other in a daze. We're tired. I'm counting the hours until our little cherubs go to sleep! I read stories to the boys while Steve plays a game with Jenna. That lasts for ten minutes, and we move on to something else. Music! Alex and his music. He's so funny. He loves anything that has music come out of it. His favorite toy is the Leap Frog Train that does several activities. He just keeps hitting the buttons and listening to the sounds. Austin, on the other hand, is just as happy as a clam crawling everywhere. He never stays in one spot for too long. He comes over by me to grab my hands, claps them together, and then crawls away. He's a hoot!! I swear Jenna is going to be a gymnast the way she jumps and twirls and flips—off the furniture, that is. A million times told— "Do not jump on our furniture, please!!"

A defiant "Nope" comes out of her precious little mouth. Did I really just say I loved how strong-willed she is?

It's getting late, and Steve needs to go downstairs to his office and get some work done. The assembly line begins! Change clothes, diapers, go potty, brush teeth, and off to la-la land! Well, two out of three kids are easy. Jenna takes a little more work. Thirty minutes go by, and, finally, she's in bed. Kisses, hugs and hopes for better tomorrows! I sit for a minute to catch my breath. I have wash to do, and so much more, but not tonight. Tomorrow is a new day!

It's 9:30 PM, and my boys are still up. I go in to check on them and they both are messing around. They love to steal each other's blankets through their crib slats. Austin thinks I've come in to chase him around the crib, and Alex is just standing there leaning, as if to say, "Hey Mom, what's up?" Put both boys back down at least another six times before they fall asleep. Well, if anything, I get my exercise chasing them around and running up and down the stairs. I also get to catch up on conversations with my husband Steve.

It's after 10 PM, and I'm beat. Another day in the life of me has completed! I've made it without pulling my hair out or crazy mood swings. Since becoming a mom, I've changed dramatically. My once fun-loving, carefree attitude has turned into more of a "drill sergeant" persona. My husband misses that part of me. So do I, believe me. Our lives are on schedules due to our boys' health issues and disabilities. But hey, that's okay. That's who we are at this phase of our lives. I love being home with my kids. I am blessed with that choice. As hard as it is financially on our family, and emotionally on me, we would not have it any other way. These are the precious and priceless times of our children's lives, and I'm so thrilled to have the opportunity to help shape these little children into the people they will become. My mom stayed home with my sister and me. That's what I remember as a child—being on the go, playing with the neighborhood kids, and just enjoying life. I hope I am bringing the same values to my children. I know I need to lighten up in some areas of our life. Life is a learning process. It's constantly changing. I like to think that, as a mom, we change too. We learn from our mistakes and strive for the best. My motto as of late has been "You live, learn, and you move forward." Also, "You can't change what you can't control!"

My family means the world to me. I thank my lucky stars every day that I was picked to be a wife to my fabulous husband and mommy to the most precious gifts in my life—Jenna, Alexander, and Austin!

A Typical Day

Elizabeth D, 31, Colorado
Military mother of one

Elizabeth, a "slightly transient Air Force spouse" and mom of one (age 2), is pregnant with her second child. A former high teacher who is a "teacher at heart," she plans to return to the classroom someday. "Being a mama changes you, but not so you become unrecognizable to yourself or others!"

4:30 AM Maddie is up. Not sure why or how this is possible. This hasn't happened in months and I stayed up way too late to manage this mystery crisis. I go in and get her, and naively lie down in the guest room with her to try and fall back asleep. Ha. I doze off a little here and there, but Maddie is poking me, tickling me, and giggling for the next two hours.

6:45 AM The day officially begins. I grumpily get out of bed and grouch at Matt (my husband), who is on his way out for work. He politely points out that at least I can keep my pajamas on for a while. True.

7:00 AM Maddie and I have breakfast. She is really getting good at eating cereal with milk. I almost knock my juice over and she says "Careful, Mama!"

7:45 AM I ambitiously decide to go upstairs and get an early shower so Maddie and I can run a few errands before playgroup. I should pack up and get ready for our walk, but something about getting up at 4:30 AM makes me want to skip it today.

8:00 AM I decide to lie down on the bed just for a few minutes while Maddie plays. Not a nap, mind you, just a "lie-down."

8:30–9:30 AM Maddie crawls up onto the bed and sacks out with me. I guess getting up at 4:30 AM doesn't suit her particularly well either. What a pleasant nap—she quit napping with me a year ago. I miss those days of bringing an immobile baby to bed for cuddling.

9:30 AM We both wake up and lay on the bed for awhile poking, tickling, and giggling wit each other. I'm a lot more amenable to this at 9:30 AM than I am pre-sunrise.

10:00 AM Time for a shower. I do a quick security sweep of the upstairs to make sure Maddie won't have anything to get into while I'm in the shower. My nightstand drawer needs to be on top of the dresser, the guest bathroom door shut, everything on the bathroom counter pushed back two feet. Somehow she still manages to get into something on most days. However, I am not willing to take my shower prior to 6:30 AM. Someone said I would turn into a morning person when she was born. Ha.

10:20 AM Make a quick call to Nicole to make sure playgroup is in the same place as last week. This wouldn't be necessary if our regular park hadn't been burned to the ground by teenaged vandals. We are bitter. Maddie takes all her clothes out of her drawers and heaps them in a pile while I am on the phone. She tells me she is being helpful. I thank her with slightly clenched teeth while I put everything away.

11:15 AM Throw lunch together for the park and initiate the 15-minute process of getting out of the house. Hat? Check. Sunglasses? Check. Extra diaper in the backpack? Check. Shoes on? Chase Maddie around while she giggles in glee as she runs away from me while I try to corner her to put shoes on. Check. Sippy cup? Check. Cell phone? Check. Keys? Keys? Keys? Check. There has to be a better way to get out of the house, I think.

11:30 AM - 1:00 PM Playgroup. I love playgroup. Maddie loves playgroup. My friends love playgroup. It is sacred time, not to be double-booked with dentist appointments, grocery shopping, or similar mundane activities. We get cranky if we have to miss a week. Maddie has a great time running around the park with her friends. I have a great time watching her while talking to my friends. We are reluctant to leave for naptime.

1:15 PM Maddie naps. I fight a nap. I go outside to continue catching up with people who must believe me to be lost at sea or dead. I am finally emerging, marginally, from the Land of The First Trimester, Round 2, where every spare minute was spent sleeping or in a sleeping position. My friends are concerned that I have disappeared, and my naturally industrious nature is sluggish while I look at the piles of unfinished projects I've neglected over the past few months. How is it that I am so much more tired this time around? I refuse to believe that a daily routine with a toddler can tire me out as equally as teaching history to 150 high school students. Today, however, I will fight the nap and at least finish up my letter to Stacey and plan my circle journal entry for the month.

3:30 PM Maddie is up; after a quick snack of "Food of the Gods" (raisins, Goldfish(r) crackers and milk), we head to Target to do the shopping we were meant to finish this morning. It is a blessing and a curse to have Super Target 45 seconds from our house in a town where it takes at least 15 minutes to get almost anywhere else. I think a little bell rings at Super Target every time I walk in, as they know that I will forget everything I went there for and come out with $87 of merchandise I didn't know I needed. True to form once again.

4:30 PM Home. I'm awake, Maddie is dancing to her favorite "They Might Be Giants" CD, and I decide for the second time today to be ambitious: I start dinner. Matt will be surprised, as he usually is when I try to cook. Despite the fact I have seven things in my repertoire that I can make with a decent amount of consistency, cooking is not my thing. I congratulate myself for the 1,756th time for planning ahead nicely by marrying someone who actually enjoys cooking.

5:15 PM Matt is home early. We like living in Colorado Springs most of the time, but we don't like the traffic. Normal get-home time for him is 5:45 PM or so.

5:45 PM Dinner. My meal is definitely edible, though I feel as if I may have exhausted my cooking quota for the week. It is not a task that comes easily to me. We sit at the table as we do almost every night, a lovely unexpected benefit of having a child. Matt and I used to eat dinner more often than not in front of the TV, but now it is just easier to catch the mess of eating with Maddie while corralled around the dining room table. Maddie chats about birds, milk, fire trucks, and her friends at the park while Matt and I catch up partially on the day's events.

6:30 PM Bedtime routine begins. Tonight is bath night, so Matt whisks Maddie upstairs to give her a "Daddy Scrub." Matt prefers this task so I happily step aside and clean up the kitchen instead. There is something pleasant about cleaning up things that don't squirm when I apply soap and water. Sounds of fun waft down from upstairs while I clean up downstairs. The kitchen looks half-cleaned up when I am finished, but, as I've used up my ambition for the day, I leave it at that.

7:09 PM "Mama!!!!!!!! STORYTIME!!!!!!!!" Matt has trained Maddie to shout at the top of her lungs when it's time for me to come upstairs for stories. She picks the books; we read them to her. This is a child who loves books. She stands in front of the bookshelf with her head cocked to the side making an indecisive 'hmmmm' sound and it melts our hearts. I can't believe I was actually worried before she was born that she wouldn't like books. The family addiction to books is thoroughly guaranteed for another generation, obviously.

7:30-ish PM Matt and I flop on the bed in a semi-stupor, talking some more about the day's events. I have a friend whose child is up until 10:00 PM or 11:00 PM every night. I do not understand this as I am so ready to put Maddie to bed by 7:00 PM and savor the remaining time in the day in relative peace and quiet. Since the beginning of this new pregnancy, this post-Maddie bedtime/pre-my bedtime is even more important since I can't stay awake much past 9:30 PM lately. I wonder if the days of staying up until midnight or 1:00 AM, working in my studio will ever come back. Surely they will...surely...

7:50 PM Matt heads downstairs to watch TV, I head out to do my long-practiced ritual of piddling around the house—a mixture of picking things up, organizing, and woolgathering. It is a comforting routine I have engaged in since my youth.

9:00 PM PJs on, face washed, teeth brushed, ready for

bed. I settle in with The Little Friend by Donna Tartt for about 30 minutes. I've let a lot of old habits go since becoming a mama, but not reading. I fall asleep with the light on before Matt comes up to bed.

Works for Us

Samantha G, 33, Southern California
Sometimes frazzled mother of three

Samantha, a married mother of three (ages 12, 5, and 21/2), describes herself as outgoing, open-minded, and free-spirited. "I love to seek and acquire knowledge. Research is my comfort zone. I love to have a noble purpose. And, I love my red (auburn, really) hair." Splitting her time between motherhood and freelance writing, she strives to better herself through her personal interest in culinary arts, gardening, and reading. "I also strive to find a benevolent common denominator between spirituality religion and faith."

2:40 AM She's right on time again, and she wants her milk. You might think I am talking about a newborn waking up for a feeding. No, I am talking about my two-and-a-half-year-old daughter, Zoë Penelope, who hogs our California king every night. Also in the California king of the so-called master suite, Alexander, our five-year-old; my husband Pete and the dog who is snoring happily on her new cushy bed from Costco. Our family bed has gone far past our initial time expectations. But tonight, tonight we are putting them in their own beds, for sure.

As usual, she greedily drains the sippy cup of "choco", or, reduced fat chocolate milk. Nesquik, to be exact. Alex calls it "bunny choco". Try to get a generic brand past their jaded taste buds, and you will be hastily reminded that toddlers are brand specific. I suppose I have no room to talk, either. It's not material, it's comfort. Comfort helps at 2:40 AM

7:30 AM Zoë is moving and grooving. I suppose I could get up now, too. Alex is still sleeping peacefully and beautifully. In fact, if you look at the back of his head while he is asleep; he still looks like a baby. I kiss his head and smell his hair (I still use Johnson's on him; comfort helps a mom, anytime). "Wiggle Bay, Momma!" Zoë wants to watch her favorite video, Wiggle Bay. As I shuffle to the bathroom, I turn on the TV and Jeff, Murray, Anthony and Greg start to sing.

9:00 AM Alex and Zoë are getting out of bed after drinking their morning "choco" and I am all dressed, hair in a clip, SPF makeup on and even lipstick that will surely be fading shortly. Alex asks what we are going to do today. Selfishly, I acknowledge that it is all dependent on my whims, since I have no major commitments pending. Maybe the park? No, it's too hot. Armstrong Garden Center? No, shopping is a nightmare with the two of them. Hmm. This requires more thought. I sit down on the couch and the two monkeys immediately fight over who gets to lie next to me, on me, in my lap or under my arm. After they work it out, I drink my coffee in two gulps. "Let's go to the park, but you have to take a bath as soon as we get home." It's a shaded park; I've got enough cash for a Starbucks on the way home.

10:00 AM The dog has fresh water and she's outside, just refilled the sippy cups with "choco", put stamps on the bills; and we're out the door. They tell me to put on their CD of compiled songs I made before downloading requiring legislation. We're listening to "yo-ho", the song from the ride, the ride of all time, Pirates of the Caribbean. Now that I am 33, I finally know all the words. I've only been to Disneyland half a million times since I was born. The lyrics have been a mystery since grade school when my junior high took an annual trip. My kids will be making said trip in a few years themselves.

Not too dirty, but overly playful, Zoë has decided to stand at the top of the big slide so we don't have to leave. Every time I climb up to get her, she goes down the slide. I climb down, she runs right back up to the slide from a different direction. Son of a bitch. We could do this all day, and that is exactly her intent. Meanwhile, Alex could be getting kidnapped and what would I say? "I was chasing my other child over which I had no control." Bad mommy. Condemned-on-the-five-o'clock-news mommy. With that visual and an I-don't-care-who-hears-it yell to Alex "GET BACK OVER HERE NOW," I perform jungle gym acrobatics with vigor that surprises even me. Within five minutes, we're back in the SUV.

2:00 PM Bath time over, the two little monsters are sitting on the couch watching PBS, if I have something to say about it. "Ed, Edd & Eddy" just make me want to throw up. When Alex starts to throw a fit because his boyish nature prefers Cartoon Network, I threaten the C-SPAN punishment. You see, he is not yet old enough to change the channel. When he pisses me off, I put it on C-SPAN until I bore him into submission. Clifford, the big, red, well-adjusted dog, is comforting. Yet again, comfort is important, especially when I have to start dinner and leave them to their own devices, toys, cartoons, and a healthy snack of roasted almonds, sliced apples and pears, and baby carrots. I am proud of myself to have folded a load of laundry, and I sit down with the kids. Still, I feel guilty for not doing ten things at once. My energy level is perfectly happy to sit, however. I close my eyes in hopes of a few moments to re-charge before making dinner. Zoë closes her eyes too, and it is a good fifteen minutes before Alex starts throwing wiffle balls at my head for attention. Carefully, I lay Zoë on a blue chenille throw pillow instead of my arm, and I draw with Alex on the Etch-a-Sketch. As many emotions as I have about my little angel, all I can seem to say is "I love you." Sweet thing that he is, he never gets tired of saying "I love you too".

5:00 PM A glass of wine tonight or not? Nah, I eat twice as much when I drink wine while cooking. Take a look in the fridge, what two vegetables and protein do I serve? I fight off the urge to cook hot, buttered noodles and decide on roasted beets and a butter lettuce salad. The thick London broils I bought at Trader Joe's brown nicely in the pan once I put the glass lid on. I finish them up in the oven with the beets. All the while I have been cooking, the kids have been playing with the neighbor children, who I guess are kind of like my children too. When asked for something, I respond, "You know where it is; get it, and leave my kitchen!" with a smirk on my face. The kitchen is mommy's domain. I create, have autonomy, and get to work alone here in my culinary sanctuary. "Poppa is home," they shout in unison as the garage door opens. They have Poppa sonar. I wish I did! I could hone in on him and plan everything accordingly, but wait, that's crazy. Even though I could handle it perfectly and to everyone's benefit, I have not been granted such divine control over other human beings. That is why I accept the bare feet getting dirty on the floor of the garage as the monkeys blissfully run to greet their daddy. Should have had that glass of wine, because now they'll need another bath.

6:10 PM We all sit down to dinner. I shovel food into my mouth at Mach 2, but the kids and hubby take their time. I get the dishes done while we all talk about our day. Worcestershire sauce is flying and diet, caffeine-free root beer is exploding out of the sippy cup spout onto the floor. It scares the dog away, so Zoë can finish most of her "steakie wakie." (Most of it ends up on the floor anyway.)

6:47-ish PM Back to the bath again. They scream for cold water, but I know what that means. Like sharks in a feeding frenzy, cold water makes the kids behave madly, with the depraved indifference of a criminal suspect. Water on the floor. More than once I have slipped and ended up on the bathroom floor in pain, moaning, but also thinking that that must have been funny. Even funnier, I am as clumsy as my own mother.

JUST ABOUT 8:00 PM Close enough to bedtime to just go to bed. Alex is nestled up against me in bed, drinking his "choco" while Poppa picks out his clothes for the next day. Zoë tries on all of his shoes. This is the time of day when hubby and I say to each other—sometimes articulately, sometimes with a wink or smile, and sometimes with the desire for a more orderly lifestyle —"This is loud! This is crazy! This is fun!" Other parents may have their kids in their own beds with teeth brushed, but this is our home and our family. It works for us. Zoë and Poppa get into bed, and, watching Wiggle Bay, The Best of Elmo, or "Baby Shake" (Zoë's name for Baby Shakespeare); we set the timer on the cable box and say our "I love you's." I'm tired. What time is it, honey? Timer goes off. Nestle in, get comfortable.

Transitions

Kimberly J, 35, Southern California
Transforming mother of one

Kimberly, a mother of one (age 1), entered into parenthood with much thought and decision. "Becoming a parent was not something I took lightly, nor did my husband. We decided to spend the first few years of our marriage just enjoying being married. Gradually, however, we started noticing how much we wanted kids. It crept up on us slowly at first, but then went full throttle. It did not happen as quickly as we would have liked, and we hit some pretty painful bumps along the journey. In the end, though, there were finally two beautiful blue lines on the EPT stick and soon enough baby made three." Retaining her sense of humor, Kimberly jokes "In my spare time (ha-ha), I enjoy spending time with friends, creative writing, reading and travel. Parenthood has also increased my interest in wine tasting."

My day begins at 4:00 AM, because Mike has to catch an early morning flight to San Jose. Before we had Connor, I used to feel really badly for my husband with his hectic travel schedule and crazy hours. Now I just envy him. I would love to get away for a few days even if it were for work and required me to get up at 4 AM. Even though he is so quiet when he gets up early, I still can never go back to sleep. Insomnia and anxiety set in when I think about how I'll be woken in just two hours anyhow or how I am going to make it through the week without Mike or what my workload will be like this week. The worst thoughts that haunt me without fail every time I have insomnia involve all the potential dangers that lurk out there, ready and waiting to harm Connor. I am sure there has to be a loose button somewhere on the carpet that he will choke on, or that one of us will slip and forget to close the baby gate in our haze of sleep deprivation, or a dresser that is not securely fastened or properly baby-proofed will tip over when he tries to scale it. It is when I think of these things that I am overcome by simultaneous feelings of and resentment. I am truly overwhelmed at the realization that I will never be free from worry now that I am a parent.

Sure enough, after two hours of tossing and turning (Chloe, our cat, gets so annoyed that she goes under the bed), my built-in alarm clock sounds through the monitor. My head is pounding as I hurry to the nursery for my morning greeting. The headache is due in large part to the combination of wine consumed last evening and the lack of sleep. I need to acknowledge the fact that three glasses of wine and motherhood simply do not mix! The problem is that it is such a rarity to have an evening out with the girls these days that I just get carried away with my freedom.

Connor greets me from his crib in the usual manner by tossing his binky at me and flashing his handsome grin. As always, he has somehow managed to become even more adorable overnight. I carry him back to the bedroom and persuade him to cuddle in bed with me for about a half hour. Chloe even comes out from under the bed to join us. "Cat!" Connor cries out and lunges toward her. I am trying to teach Connor to be gentle with Chloe and he is slowly making progress. He recently stopped pulling her tail and we are now working on the ears. Just as we are all about to doze off, Sydney, our dog, starts barking downstairs as a reminder that she cannot start her day until we all make it downstairs. "Dog!" Connor shouts out. I sigh and lift Connor out of the bed with me. Sydney is waiting for us at the bottom of the stairs with one of my Ugg slippers in her mouth (favorite pair, of course). I note that the slipper has been chewed beyond repair. It is only 6:30 AM, and I am already annoyed. I want to yell at her but I refrain as she gently jumps up to give me a big wet kiss. Chloe has now made her way downstairs and Sydney promptly starts chasing her across the kitchen. This time I do yell, very loudly, for Sydney to leave Chloe alone. Connor immediately starts crying. I try to calm him while putting out Fancy Feast for Chloe and Iams for Sydney. Once Connor is calm, I get his cereal, milk, and bananas ready. Breakfast goes okay and Connor only tosses his food at Sydney twice. I fantasize throughout breakfast about Starbucks. If only they delivered!

After breakfast I change Connor and get him ready for a stroll. I have way too much fun picking out his daily outfits. I never thought clothing for little boys would be so cute. Today I have chosen a navy blue Tommy Hilfiger onesie. I squeeze his butt cheek before putting on his diaper and make a "honk" sound. This always gets a grin from him. I think about the day he will be too old for me to squeeze his butt cheeks, and it makes me very sad. The doorbell interrupts my thoughts. I have no choice but to answer it, even though I am braless and have not combed my hair, because Sydney is barking so loudly. It is the Fed-Ex guy with a package for me from the office. He takes one look at me and apologizes, assuming he has woken me up. I tell him not to worry about it. Connor is in my arms; the Fed-Ex guy comments on what a beautiful baby I have. This should make me happy but all I can think about later is that he did not check me out, despite the fact that I was braless and in a white tee shirt. To make matters worse, he also called me ma'am—TWICE. Ever since turning 35 last month, I have entered the dreaded land of ma'am. I'm sure the perpetual bags under my eyes don't help.

As Connor plays with his Legos, I check myself out in the mirror, while putting on my staple stay-at-home mom outfit (striped Adidas pants, tee shirt and baseball hat). There is no disputing that pregnancy and nursing have made my boobs saggy or that I am still carrying around an extra five pounds. It has been one year since I had Connor and I am still waiting for my body to return to me. I suppose diet and exercise would help but who has the time. I think about how my nickname in college was "the body" and now I am a viable candidate for a reality makeover TV show. It makes me want to cry. In fact, if Sydney wasn't waiting patiently downstairs for her walk and starting her slow agonized groan, I would probably sit down and cry my eyes out. Cry over the fact I have had nothing but sporadic interest in sex since getting pregnant and giving birth. Cry over the constant state of sleep deprivation both Mike and I have lived under for one year. Cry about the dog and cat hair lining our furniture, the sticky kitchen floor, the laundry, the dirty dishes, the bills, the unanswered phone calls and email. Cry about how I never have enough time to get my work done and that makes me feel as if I am drowning. Cry about how much I miss reading books that aren't about parenthood, taking bubble baths, sleeping late, going to happy hour with my friends, and having dinner and movie nights with Mike. Cry about how I know I won't ever feel good about my body again. Cry about my recent revelation that I feel too old and tired to ever have another baby. Then the guilt sets in, as it always does, reminding me of what a blessing Connor is and how I should be enjoying every minute of parenthood.

I snap out of it and round up Connor and Sydney for our morning stroll. It is a beautiful day and we head toward the park. The park does not allow dogs (even leashed) but we conveniently ignore this rule. Connor reaches his hand out from his stroller to help me hold Sydney's leash. It is such an endearing gesture, one of millions I have witnessed from him this past year, and I am truly taken aback at what an amazing little boy I have.

After our walk, I give Connor his mid-morning meal and get us ready for Gymboree class. For once, we actually leave the house on time. However, it ends up taking us double the normal amount of time to get there because I am unaware that today is the opening day of the Del Mar Races, an event that used to be the epicenter of my social life. Fortunately, Connor travels pretty well and keeps himself busy by flipping through his touch-n-feel animal book. As we pass the track, I recall many previous opening days where my girlfriends and I would get decked out in cute dresses, hats, and purses and take a limo to the track. We would drink martinis and choose which horses to bet on based on the surefire method of selecting the one with the cutest name to win. We would end the day having dinner down by the water. I look again in the rearview mirror at Connor, who is now starting to doze off, thanks to the traffic, and think about how different my life is now. I haven't been to opening day at the races in three years (including today). Three years ago, I was undergoing exploratory surgery to find out why I could not conceive. Last summer, we had just brought the little guy home from the hospital (turns out we could conceive after all, something I will always be grateful for until the day I die). Now here I am on my way to a class that annoys the crap out of me, rather than boozing it up at the track. I do so with a smile on my face though because, if one thing is certain, Connor loves his Gymboree class. Besides, isn't part of motherhood the willingness to make an ass out of oneself every now and then?

To be fair, it's not so much the class that bugs me; rather, if I am completely honest, it is my lack of vocal skills or rhythm. Yes, Gymboree is my worst nightmare come true. I have to actually sing and dance for an hour. I am the one whose friends all called her immediately after the famous Seinfeld episode where Elaine tried to dance. "You were just on TV!" they all howled into the phone, laughing hysterically. Obviously, Gymboree is not about me but it is a bit embarrassing. Class today goes okay. We start with a topic discussion on the biggest challenge we are currently facing in regard to parenting. Several women discuss problems with their babies not sleeping through the night. We all nod ours heads empathetically. Even the women who have little angels who sleep through the night nod their heads in a knowing manner because they are smart in their assumption that it's best if they never admit this to anyone. One of the other mothers talks about how guilty she feels now that she has two children because there never seems to be enough time for both. She breaks into tears and I feel awful for her. Another woman has a husband in Iraq and has not seen him for six months. It's one thing to survive without my husband a few nights a week, but I cannot even fathom having the strength and energy to do this all alone month after month.

After the discussion, it's music time. Yet again, I sing completely off-key to all the lyrics and cannot dance in step with the other moms. Connor does not seem to notice though or, if he does notice, he apparently doesn't care because he has a big grin on his face the whole time. On second thought, maybe he is actually having a good chuckle at his mom's expense. He is pretty advanced for his age, after all, and can probably see Mom has no future in the music industry. As I drive us home, I think about the group discussion and how lucky I am. All I could talk about is how frustrating it's been lately to work from home even though it is supposed to be an ideal situation (or so I tell everyone).

Connor has his lunch once we are home and then goes down for his nap. The beauty of him now only napping once per day is that it is a jumbo nap and allows me to squeeze in about two-and-a-half to three hours of uninterrupted work. Today this is essential because my "part-time" job is starting to add up to more than 20 hours per week. I cannot complain because I am so fortunate to be able to work from home and to be home with Connor for the past year. Yet not so fortunate when I think of the logistical challenges of working from home, as when Sydney started barking in the background when I was conducting an international phone interview. Then there was the time the cleaning lady started vacuuming right outside of my home office, after our babysitter had already knocked on my office door and asked where the sunscreen for Connor was because they were going to the park, all as I was on a conference call with a company VP. He commented on how my office sounded like Grand Central Station. I worried for weeks they'd make me give up telecommuting and return to the office. I worried because I knew deep down inside (despite all those adamant proclamations made over the year, and always after a really bad day, that I WOULD RETURN TO THE OFFICE, NO MATTER WHAT, ONCE CONNOR TURNED ONE) I was not ready to leave him. I'm still not sure when I will be.

Two hours and forty-five minutes later, I hear Connor turning on his Ocean Wonders Aquarium sound machine. I greedily try to pound out one last email before heading upstairs. He is still a bit groggy, and it is perfect time to cuddle. We snuggle up on the sofa, Sydney at our feet, and watch a Baby Einstein video until it is time for dinner. As always, Mike checks in at 5 PM sharp to see how everyone is doing, even though he is rushing from a late afternoon meeting to a dinner meeting. I tell Connor "Da Da" is one the phone. He takes the phone from my hand and tries to eat it. Mike is eager to hear all the Connor stories from the day. I knew my husband would be a good father but I really had no concept as to the magnitude of his commitment to fatherhood, his absolute enjoyment and delight in it, and his unending patience. I wish I could absorb some of his patience through osmosis. It is because I am thinking of these things that I decide not to bitch about the fact that he is dining at Ruth's Chris Steak House this evening and I will be lucky if Connor shares some of his pasta pickups with me. By the way, one of the most ironic things about motherhood is that you never have time to eat, yet you never lose weight.

After dinner I pack up Connor and tell him we are meeting Gram Gram for coffee. Better late than never on the Starbucks. It is an awkward meeting because my mom and I have not spoken in two weeks over the fact that she would not take a day off from work to watch Connor for me when I came down with strep-throat and Mike was out of town for work. It is one of many such disagreements we have had since Connor was born, about her definition of a grandmother versus mine. Although I think most mother-daughter relationships are strengthened when the daughter becomes a mother herself, ours has actually deteriorated, sadly enough. Although we may never see eye to eye on this issue, and it has certainly cost us a lot in terms of our own relationship, we have at least been smart enough to not let it affect Connor.

I decide to break the ice by telling her how annoyed I am at Pottery Barn for Kids because Connor did not win the baby-of-month contest. She agrees to boycott Pottery Barn altogether. Connor is happy to see her and I am glad he is too young to pick up on any drama. We keep the conversation light and catch up on work and family gossip over mochas. At one point, Connor reaches for my hand with his right hand and, at the same time, grabs my Mom's hand with left. He then does something I can barely believe—he takes our hands and places them together. We both smile, and I realize why the name Connor means "wise."

When we return home, it is time for the bedtime ritual. Connor loves his tubby time and it is hard to get him out. He kicks and screams as I try to get him into his diaper and pajamas. The same goes for his bottle. I long for the days when things like bedtime bottles and diaper changes used to be relatively calm events. As he is so worked up by the time I put him down, I stay in the room with him until he falls asleep. He has this habit of wanting to hold my hand until he drifts off. I have been informed—ad nauseam—by every person in the world, and almost all parenting books on the market, what a horrible habit this is. Tonight I eschew all such advice and he is asleep within 15 minutes. I blow him a kiss and whisper how much I love him before tiptoeing out. It is 8:30 PM and my options are endless. I have about an hour and half before bed. I can check emails or return phone personal calls. I should probably spend some time with Sydney and there is certainly some laundry that needs to be folded. On second thought, it's been a really long day and I think I'll just draw myself a hot bath.

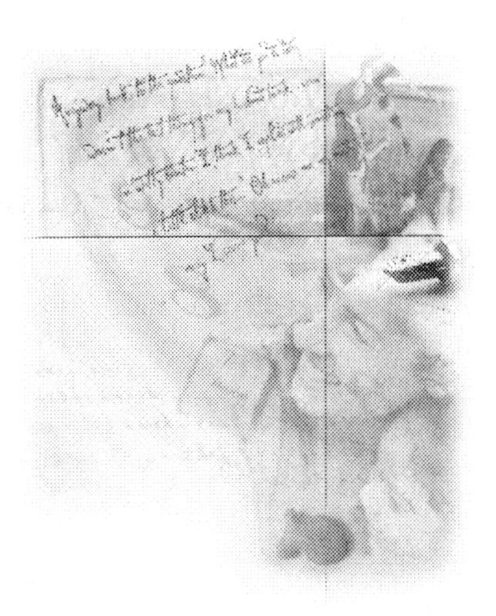

"...For Better, For Worse, For Richer, For Poorer, In Sickness and In Health..."

When the world says, "Give up," Hope whispers, "Try it one more time."
~ Author Unknown

...Help!! My 13-year-old stepson has gone from a well-behaved boy to a juvenile delinquent. He is constantly breaking the rules, lying, and more. My husband wants to sit down and have a talk with him this afternoon, but I'm scared. Will he resent me? I already feel like I'm just a stranger to him. When my husband and I got married two years ago, I thought I'd have this great relationship with my stepson. For awhile, I did. Then it all changed. I don't want to be the bad "guy" here, but I'm sure I will be since I'm the step-parent. I had no idea being a step-parent would be this hard. Now, I'm re-thinking my wish to have my own child. I don't want the baby to grow up and hate me like my stepson does.

~ Stacie N, 32, Texas
Scared step-mom of two (ages 13 and 8)

9:01 AM Today I'm visiting my dad at the nursing home. I never know if he is going to remember who I am—let alone who his grandchildren are. His Alzheimer's is getting progressively worse each visit. I feel like he's my new baby. It's all I can do not to cry throughout each visit.

~ Ellen P, 44, New York
Divorced mother of three (ages 12, 15, and 17)

I have a long day ahead of me. My daughter, lil' Cindy, has been sick the last couple of days due to weather changes, and I have counseling. I attend trauma counseling due to several things that happened during my childhood and youth. My mother passed away at 38, and I was raised in the carnival most of my life. I have taken plenty of parenting classes to undo the wasted life styles that were taught to me. Nothing, though, has prepared me for mommyhood. It is a wonderful and blessed gift that can tell a thousand stories to make you laugh, cry, and just be dumbfounded.

~ Tonya S, 26, Washington
Thriving mother of one (age 2)

4:34 PM I have a very spirited daughter, and at time I feel like I'm at my wits end some days. Today is one of those days. I am counting the minutes until my husband comes home. Anyway, I feel like a total failure as a mom right now. I've been sitting in the bathroom crying my eyes out. I try to vent with my husband, but he doesn't really understand since he's at work most of the day and not with our daughter. Still, as difficult as she is, I wouldn't trade her for anything in the world.

~ Tina K, 30, Pennsylvania
Struggling mom of one (age 4)

My husband just admitted that he isn't happy anymore. I don't get it. I do everything for him. I make his meals, do his laundry —how can he not be happy with me when he's never even here. He's always with his friends. I know that we are young. I got pregnant after we'd only been dating for a few months. I miss having all the fun I used to, but we have a baby now. Isn't it supposed to get easier after you have a baby and get married?

~ Felicity D, 21, Nevada
Young mother of one (age 1)

5:05 PM Sam is crying again. My mom calls this the bewitching hour. I call it hell. If it only lasted an hour, I'd be fine. However, Sam seems to cry for hours on end. My sister says it is just colic and he should outgrow it by four months. Four months!? He's only four weeks now!

~ Ann D, 29, Virginia
Married mom of one (age 4 weeks)

...About two weeks ago I miscarried. I wasn't very far along—only six weeks, but it hurts just the same. It amazes me how we are able to love a being so completely without even knowing it. I think it is hardest when I look at my son and wonder if he'll ever know that he missed having this brother or sister.

~ Toni Y, 26, Northern California
Grieving mother of one (age 3)

Dear Diary,

I've never been one to worry about my health, but my pap came back abnormal. I'm sure it is nothing. However, I'm still a little worried. I need to remind my self that there is more at stake than just my life. My health affects my family too.

~ Helen W, 43, Florida
Affected mom of two (ages 11 and 9)

Weathering the Storm

Anonymous, Southern California
Mother of three

We acquire the strength we have overcome.
~ Ralph Waldo Emerson

The serenity prayer is actually the prayer of St. Francis. These are the things you can learn when you read and turn the light off then go to sleep like a normal person, instead of crying yourself to sleep or condemning yourself for being too weak to stop the insanity of "the disease".

It has been a year and a half now that "the disease" has moved into our lives and taken up residence in our previously happy home. What went wrong? At 35 years old, why did he choose controlled substances over "happily ever after?" Mr. Clean Cut, rise to the occasion, charming as can be, ends up in the can weighing in at one hundred and forty pounds (that's less than me, you bastard). Take your "for better or for worse" to your shallow grave after your lethal dose, that's how much I feel for you, baby. You brought this into our home. The kids could have reached into your wallet, curious as they are, and there ends the symphonic beat of the beautiful hearts we created.

It is not me that saved them, no. That was divine intervention. Cleaning up the mess and the residuals is left to us, the "adults". The divine intervention here is free will, which is part of my problem. It is more than half the time now that I believe I am not up for the job.

I can't leave, you won't go, and I will be damned before I set one foot back in family court. And the kids, I suppose I damn them too with my failure to act. I don't deserve to be their mother, or anyone's mother, for that matter. Self-indulgent, resentful, and emphatically pessimistic, I am not even the pretty mess I was in my twenties. What I am now is the woman you love to condemn, because I make forgiving, average misgivings, acceptable. I am not an accomplice to my husband's addiction and lies. I am a criminal, too, because my anger has become my personality.

So, speaking of divinity, I wonder what I am supposed to learn, seek, or gain from this adversity. If everything happens for a reason, as I have always believed, what good can possibly come from this? That my kids enter Al-A-Teen before high school? The damage done to my babies is unforgivable. I give them all the love I can. I reassure them, I hold them, and I listen and respond carefully, not dismissively. I take them out everyday so you can "look for jobs on the internet". Five months out of work, and I am supposed to be patient. I am supposed to not only make sacrifices but also to have no human emotions. Oh, okay, I am allowed to have human emotions but I am not supposed to express myself like a lunatic. Uh-oh, I'm no longer neurotic in a cute way; I am, what is it you told me at three o'clock in the morning, bipolar?

I don't believe it. That's the shred of strength I have left. In my journal, in my pillow where I scream and cry, I will tell myself I can't do this. It's over. I gave it my best shot, and the kids will recover. My instinct tells me no, though. I won't do that to them, not yet.

I love them so much. I love you. Come back from where you have been. It's cold outside, and they don't know you like I do. Never in a million years could anyone else understand us. But it is undeniable that we are a family, and I'll keep fighting for our sacred share of heaven on earth; the twinkle in their eyes, the resolution of an embrace. We are who we are, no apologies, no explanations. Everything we need is right here.

The kids are chasing the dog again, they're laughing so loud and breathlessly that it almost sounds like crying. They are so happy; you should come and see.

Something More

Darcy M, 25, Kansas
Wondering mother of two

"I'm a secretary for a marketing executive. I was born and raised in Kansas. Sometimes I wish we could move somewhere else. It seems like there has to be more out there," ponders Darcy, married mother of two (ages 5 and 3). Finding strength with her relationship with God, she admits she is confused by His plan. "I wonder if God has a special plan for me, or is this it? I feel ashamed about this, but I sometimes question His plan. Is there something more than this for me?"

Dear Diary,

Today started out just like any other day. I woke up at 5:30 AM and hopped in the shower before the kids woke. As I was drying off, my five-year-old daughter came in. She snuggled under our covers watching cartoons until I finished getting ready for work. I woke my three-year-old son and got him dressed. He resisted any attempts at being anything but a toddler. After our usual breakfast on-the-go of bagels, cream cheese and jelly, I dropped the kids off at daycare. I rushed to work arriving a little after 8:00 AM. Luckily, my boss wasn't there, so he didn't see me arrive late. Being his secretary is a bit like being a mother. He expects me to be at his beck and call; I pick up his messes and correct his mistakes. Anyway, the day was fairly uneventful. I was late picking up the kids from daycare again, because I had to stay until my boss returned from his last meeting. After we all got home, I made macaroni and cheese. Afterwards, I sat down to play with the kids. My son told me that he wanted a new mommy, and he wanted a new one now. Wow. That hurt so much. I tried not to cry, but I couldn't help it. This was my little boy who showered me with love and attention just a few weeks ago. What had I done to make him not love me anymore? Yes, I'm working a lot more, but we need the money. My husband's job isn't that secure. He doesn't know if he'd be laid off or not. I admit that the last thing I want to do at the end of the day is read Goodnight Moon or another Barney story at least 20 times. Maybe this is why he's mad. It is so much easier to pop in a video and zone out. I feel like the world's worst mother. In fact, my son wouldn't even let me put him to bed tonight. My husband had to do it. So, here I sit writing all this down with a Kleenex in my hand to dab away the tears. How come motherhood always looks so easy when other people are doing it? There is the mom down the street with four kids who all seem perfect. She gets to stay home with them. Maybe that is the difference. I don't know. I also just read "People" magazine showing all the new moms in Hollywood. Their days look so simple. When will my life get easier? I shouldn't complain, but tonight just really got to me. As I say my evening prayer tonight, I'll thank God for my family, but I'll also ask for a better tomorrow.

Homeless and Hidden

Rachel*, 26, Southern California
Single mother of one

Rachel* is a homeless mother of one (age 3) living in San Diego. She left an abusive relationship, taking with her, Tommy*, her son and just a few belongings. On occasion she is able to find temporary housing, but she and her son are usually without a roof over their heads. I first noticed Rachel and Tommy, not because I saw them but because I noticed their shopping cart. It was full of dirty blankets, a folded-up stroller, a tattered teddy bear and a few other toys. I soon found the two of them close by. Rachel was standing in the parking lot of the grocery store which is sandwiched between the luxury hotels and high-rise condominiums. Her son stood close beside her with his head hung low, watching an army of ants march by. Shopper after shopper walked by them; each passerby was careful to avoid making eye-contact. I approached Rachel and asked if she'd like to share her story. In exchange for anonymity and a meal for the two of them, she agreed to tell me about a day in her life. "I just want people to know I'm just like them too when it comes to lovin' my son."

I woke up early today. Before the sun was up, I think. I don't know what time it was, because I don't have a watch. The first thing I always do is make sure Tommy is okay. He is sleeping next to me. He looks like he is dreaming. He has a kind of smile on his face. I don't get to see that too much anymore, so I just look at him for awhile. We was lucky last night. There was room

*Names changed to protect their identity

at the mission for us. When we can find a room, it usually means we can have something to eat for breakfast.

Usually when I wake up in those places, I just lay on the bed and think and listen. I hear a lot of whispers and snoring too. There was a man last night that was so loud I thought the roof would cave in. This morning after I woke up and was holding Tommy, I thought about donuts. I always hope for donuts, because my boy loves donuts. I wish he could have all the donuts in the world. I think a lot about what life might be like if I could buy donuts all the time. I also think about turning off the lights. There are always lights on somewhere at these places.

After Tommy wakes up, we get in line for breakfast. We get some oatmeal and bread but I don't see any donuts. I tell Tommy I'm sorry. He just looks at me with those big, brown eyes. He never complains. I don't think he remembers his life being any other way. He was only a baby—just turned one—when we left.

After we ate, we got moving. I like to always be moving and keeping busy. If we are just sitting, I start to get sad. We was coming over here to the grocery store because there is a man here who will give us something to eat and drink. That's where you found me. So here I am eating sandwiches at the park with you. Tommy likes coming to the park. I do too. It makes me feel like we're "normal." People sometimes say "hi" to us when we are here. Other times people just ignore us. I know we don't smell very good and our clothes aren't nice, but we are good people. We don't get to shower all the time. People look at me like I'm hurting my son. I'm not. I love him. I want to live in a house someday. I remember living in an apartment with my boyfriend. It was nice to have a shower there and TV. I miss TV a lot. I know Tommy would love a TV. He would like to watch all those cartoons. Instead he just watches the world. My boy may not talk a lot, but he knows a lot. He watches the world. He is smart. He is going to be something someday. I know it.

I'm not asking anyone for anything. I would never hurt anyone. But I feel like people are afraid of me. Sometimes people throw pennies at me and tell me to get a job. Tell me to get a life. They don't know how hard I try. There is no one to watch Tommy. I can't trust anyone. Sometimes I can sell blood, but can't do that too much. There's a place here that we are trying to get into. They will put Tommy in school while I can work, but I can't get in yet. I don't know why.

Sometimes people give us food just because. One time a lady gave me a can of food. It was nice, but I couldn't do much with it since I don't have a can opener. I'm sure the can is in here somewhere (she starts to dig in her shopping cart). There is also the man at the grocery store who always buys us stuff. He looks for us each week. I think he really cares. Sometimes people give us leftovers from their fancy meals. The food is good except for the salad. You learn quick that salad gives you the runs.

I didn't want a life like this. I lived in a house. I went to school. My boyfriend started hitting me. I could handle that, but I was afraid he would hurt Tommy. I couldn't handle that. No one will ever hurt my boy. I feel like I'm safe now. I know my boyfriend don't know where I am.

It isn't easy out here though. A lot of the people out here drinking and drugging, but I can't, you see. I have to stay strong for my boy. He needs his mama to be good. I never seen anyone die, but I do see a lot of fights. People fight over clothes, over food, over a park bench. We have to survive. I try to walk away. I don't want Tommy thinking that fighting is okay. I don't want him to grow up to be like his daddy.

You want to know what time of day I do things. I don't know. I don't have a watch or a clock, so I follow the sun. When the sun is up, it's daytime. When it is down, it's night. Somedays we wait in line for the social worker. Other days we just walk around. There are a few places we can go to sit down. Some of them have showers, TVs and toys for Tommy.

I like being in San Diego, because it is warm most of the year. Sometimes we can stay at the beach or a park. After the park, we will probably stop by the church. I like going to the church. I went to Catholic Church when I was a little girl. I want Tommy to know that God is with us.

Sometimes I like sleeping at the beach. Even though I know we won't wake up with breakfast, that's okay. It is nice down there, because Tommy and I can pretend we are on vacation. Sometimes we find seashells. We found a shovel and pail once, so now he can dig a lot. He loves to play in the sand. Maybe tonight that's what we'll do. It was hot today so it should be a nice night at the beach. I never sleep very well no matter what, because I have to watch out for us. But we usually feel better at the beach than in the park. When we get tired, we get our blankets and hold each other. I tell Tommy stories until he falls asleep. I think the ocean helps him go to sleep faster.

I don't know why you would want to know about my life. It isn't anything special. I don't think anyone notices me or Tommy very much. We keep to ourselves. I just want to give him more. He is such a good boy. I want him to have his own room with all the toys in the world. I want him to have friends he can come to the park with. I want him to have everything. I love him so much it hurts. He's what keeps me going. If I didn't have him, I could've started turning tricks and made enough for an apartment. But I don't want him to think his mama is a whore. I'm not. I'm a good woman. I just have a spell of bad luck.

The afternoon sun shone brightly as we said our goodbyes. I offered Rachel and Tommy a ride to the beach or the shelter. She said no. After giving them a modest donation, I watched them walk off. She was a proud mother, and her son was totally devoted to her. I have since tried to locate Rachel, but to no avail, and I can only hope that Rachel and Tommy have found a place to call home and watch cartoons to their hearts' delight. There are many Rachels and Tommys in the world. If you want to reach out to those in need, please contact the National Coalition for the Homeless for more ideas on how you can help at 202.737.6444 or www.nationalhomeless.org.

Broken Bones and a Brittle Spirit

Melinda B, 39, Southern California
Selfless mother of one

Melinda, a military wife and mother of one (age 21 months), lives in San Diego and copes with day to day life while her husband is stationed overseas. "Practicing and teaching yoga helps keep me relaxed, focused, and energized to keep up with my toddler." Also a writer and editor with over 15 years in the publishing field, she is now a regular contributor to regional and local publications as well as national magazines. A selfless, devoted wife and mother, she's the picture of thousands of military spouses who are left to be both mother and father. "Sometimes I daydream about basking in a glamorous career and escaping the toil of full-time motherhood, but I adore my son, Ross, and relish the precious days I spend with him."

Today is Sunday. Ross has finished eating a bowl of dinosaur oatmeal, which gives me a twinge of guilt when I watch him pick out the dinosaurs made of pure sugar and pop them in his mouth. But I tell myself, the oatmeal is better than the ice cream he asked for as we were walking down the stairs to the kitchen this morning. By the way, he rarely gets ice cream at all, but these days he asks for it for breakfast, lunch, and dinner.

Guilt. It's the overriding emotion of my life since Ross was born in April 2002. I glance up from the Sunday paper and see that he's glued to the TV, watching a new show on PBS called "Boobah." One mom in my playgroup described this show as "crack-cocaine for kids." Seeing the spaced-out look on his face, I can see why.

As he sits there in his TV trance, with his leg in a cast and propped up, I feel guilt tapping me on the shoulder once again.

Or maybe it never stopped, but it's simply tapping louder.

Ross is 21 months old now and has an extensive vocabulary; he knows his shapes—even a trapezoid and hexagon, which I must have known at some point but could not remember until I sat down with the shape puzzle and taught them to him ... or rather he taught them to me.

What else have I forgotten? I know that a toddler still thinks his parents are gods. What will happen when he turns 13 and realizes how little I know?

I'm sure his academic knowledge will surpass mine long before he reaches adolescence. He already knows his colors, can point out many letters in the alphabet as well as some planets in the solar system and can count to eight. I know he's smart, but the thing I love most about him is the way he can light up any room, simply by walking into it. It makes all of this guilt bearable.

I reassure myself that it's okay for him to watch one hour of morning television, and I continue looking through the San Diego Union-Tribune. After reading to see whether any helicopters have been shot down in Iraq, I peruse the "Help Wanted" section, just as I do each week.

It's nice to see what kind of jobs I could have with my MBA, marketing, and editing experience. Sometimes I daydream about hour-long lunches with the girls, solo trips to the restroom at my leisure, uninterrupted time typing at the computer, an updated wardrobe. Aaah, the glamorous life of the office worker. I miss it.

I left my job as an editor of a group of RV travel magazines when I became a mom. I continue working from home about 15 hours each week as a freelance writer. I squeeze in writing time during naps and at bedtime and conduct my interviews while Ross goes to a sitter's house two mornings each week. The pay isn't much but it's tough to beat the flexible hours.

Although it's nice to fantasize about making a decent salary and being a professional woman again, the thought of being separated from Ross 40-plus hours a week ties my stomach in knots. No more long morning cuddle times, no spontaneous trips to the zoo, no giggles before naptime, no more craft time, no more parent participation music /gymnastic classes. No paycheck could ever measure up.

Raised in a single-parent family, I feel as if I was robbed of my own childhood; I couldn't stand to miss out on Ross' childhood —no matter the financial or self-fulfilling sacrifice. That would be a burden too heavy to carry.

I know that my husband Pat is feeling that weight right now. He's helping fight the war in Iraq while I fight my own private wars here. How do I explain to Ross that his daddy isn't coming home for months while masking my own feelings of anxiety and anger? Does he hear my voice crack as we sing "Itsy Bitsy Spider" because I heard on the news that a helicopter crashed near Fallujah? Does he sense the emptiness I feel at night?

Yesterday Ross heard the gardener mowing the lawn and squealed with delight, "Daddy! Daddy!" He was certain that Pat was out front mowing the lawn, just as he had two months earlier. I agonized over whether to include the mistaken identity story in my nightly e-mail to Pat or not. Would it break his heart or reassure him that Ross hasn't forgotten him?

There are plenty of military families in worse situations than we are in. But knowing that doesn't seem to make it any easier. Pat was an active-duty Navy helicopter pilot when I first met him. We knew we wanted children and that the six-month deployments that come with the Navy would be hard on our family life.

So Pat chose to pursue a career with United Airlines and remained active in the Navy Reserves. But after 9/11, our lives changed dramatically. United Airlines, like the entire airline industry, faced financial challenges and furloughed thousands of pilots; Pat was one of them.

In March 2003, with the drums of war beating in Iraq, most of Pat's squadron was mobilized and he was sent to the Middle East. I know he has felt torn between doing what he has been trained to do and being away from his family. During his four-month absence, he missed many milestones—Ross' first steps, his first words, his first temper tantrum, his first birthday.

Those first four months dragged by and we survived the separation. Thanks to e-mail and a digital camera, I was able to keep Pat posted about all he was missing at home. Somehow I even managed to keep my own complaining at a minimum.

Just as we were getting back into a routine after his return, Pat left again in November for another four-month stint in

Baghdad. He spent Christmas in the desert, and I spent it with my sister and her family. He's been gone for most of this year, and his absence is beginning to feel normal. I'm getting used to him being gone, and that bothers me even more.

But Sundays are the loneliest days of the week for me. During the week, it's easy to fill our days with play dates, playgroups, and field trips. But most fathers are home during the weekend, and Sundays are family days for many of our friends. It's like the Kris Kristopherson song, "...there's something 'bout a Sunday, makes a body feel alone."

This Sunday I'm feeling especially alone—and bitter. Pat has no idea how difficult it is being home alone 24/7 with a toddler, much less a toddler in a cast. Earlier this month, Ross broke his leg at the playground. It happened in an instant, yet in my mind's eye the scene still plays out in slow motion.

We were at the park at playgroup and Ross was climbing up to the slide. I was standing near him and talking to another mom when I looked up and saw Ross hanging from a bar—something he picked up from gymnastics class. I knew he couldn't hang there long, so I ran (in what felt like slow motion) to grab him. I didn't make it in time and he dropped to the ground, with what looked like an easy landing.

I thought he landed on his bottom, but his leg was bent beneath him, catching the weight of his body. He had two fractures and is now in a full-leg cast.

After a trip to his pediatrician and to the hospital for X-rays, I took him to Balboa Naval Hospital for his casting. I was shaken. I was crying. I couldn't believe my little baby was hurting so badly. I needed Pat here with us. Our country needed him more.

Each time someone at the doctor's office or hospital asked me how it happened, I saw in their eyes that they were looking for signs of intentional abuse. I don't blame them and am thankful that our medical system has become more proactive in actual abuse cases, but I found myself choosing my words carefully when telling the story. I knew they were watching for red flags, and I become self-conscious—showing my true concern without being overly dramatic. That's all I needed now—an interrogation from Child Protective Services.

I peek at the notes written on Ross's medical record: "Mother and toddler interacting well with each other. Child is happy and well adjusted." I breathe a sigh of relief and realize that no one here is blaming me for his accident—except myself, of course.

Ross has been a trooper throughout this whole ordeal and even the doctor commented that he had never seen a child sit so still and be so quiet for a casting.

Now for the past couple of weeks, I've been carrying Ross—and his three-pound cast—most everywhere. But it didn't take him long to figure out how to crawl while dragging it behind him. He also discovered that it makes a great ramp for his toy cars. I'm amazed at how easily kids adapt.

When it first happened, my guilt was almost unbearable. I

thought over and over in my head what I could have done differently. Then I began blaming Pat for part of it. I rationalized that being a single parent for these months has worn me down to a nub of an inattentive mother.

Now I've stopped assigning blame and have chalked it up to one of those rites of parenthood. I'm glad that Ross has an adventuresome spirit and I don't want to squash it by hovering on top of him. I only wish I could have gotten to him a littler sooner and caught him before he fell.

All too often I find myself looking back at each stage, each day, wondering what I could have done to be a better mother. Could I have breastfed him longer when he was an infant? Did he eat enough vegetables today? Is he getting enough structure play? Enough unstructured play? Is he still hurt because I lost my cool and yelled?

It's no wonder that, as kids get older, moms begin to put guilt trips on them. We have so much to unload from our own shoulders.

If I'm not looking backward, it seems as if I'm looking forward. Today I can't stop thinking about Pat's return. I want him home with us. Tonight I make dinner, sit down to eat with Ross, clean the kitchen, put the trash on the curb, give Ross a bath, read him three books, give him a back rub, clean the toy room, then plop down in front of the computer to send Pat an e-mail.

I want to be upbeat. I want to be strong. I want to be supportive. But I'm feeling so disconnected, so exhausted, so lonely today that instead I write him a letter telling him how hard this is on me and that I feel like our marriage is falling apart. Before I send it to him, I see an e-mail message that he's sent to me. I open it and read...

"Thanks for the nice letter. You have done a great job of letting me know what's been going on back home and trying to let me share in the experience of Ross's transition from post-baby to full-on toddler. I must say when I look at those photos and read the things you've written about the things he says—I do feel like I've missed so much. It makes me sad—I'll never get that time back. But ... he will continue to change and grow and there will be other times for me to share in person. I will make time for ... you and Ross. My time away this past year has been for a good cause—but we have made personal sacrifices. As hard as it has been, I have to believe it is worth it ... and one day, Ross will understand and appreciate the sacrifices as well. Even though he remembers me being gone now ... as he grows older, I think this time will be a blur for him and he won't really remember it. You will, of course. Anyhow... I think I'll be home sooner than we thought."

In that one instant, everything turns around. I think of Pat sleeping on a wobbly cot, waking to the sound of nearby explosions and gunfire, eating crappy food, donning his chemical suit during drills, and missing his family—his son. I feel ashamed for my weakness—proud of my husband's strength. But mostly I feel excited for him to come home and for the three of us to be together again.

A Missing Piece of the Family Puzzle

Lisa A, 38, North Carolina
Longing mother of two

Lisa, a "single" married mother of two (ages 5 and 20 months), who lives North Carolina, endures a long and trying separation from her husband. An active mom who also works as a software engineer, she admits that she is not superwoman. She is a person. Through it all, she maintains her wit and zeal for life through her tenacious devotion to her family.

It is 12:30 in the morning. I have finished my homework for my online class. Thank God for online classes! With two kids, a full-time job and being a single mother for all intended purposes there is no other way I could finish my Bachelor's degree. My husband has returned to his home country due to J1 Visa issues. We have been dealing with the INS since February of 2003. He left when our youngest was four months old. My five-year-old and 22-month-old are sleeping (for now). I am just now getting a chance to catch my breath after returning from our vacation.

My youngest child's daycare was closed for a week and, to avoid paying another $240 for his care for the week, I took a week's vacation. What a business childcare is! I pay more for child care than I do for my mortgage. I flew with the kids to my family's home in Illinois. With the youngest being one, it would be the last time that he could fly for free. Can you believe that the airlines charge a full price fare for a child over two-years-old? That is completely insane.

It is said that hindsight is 20-20 and, now, I would say that I would have been better off staying at home for the week. I was born in the small town that we visited. This trip was the first trip that I actually returned to the hospital where I was born. Not for reminiscing, of course. Our first visit occurred on the day after we arrived. My youngest had an ear infection. It was his first since February. The next trip to the hospital was at 2 AM, three days into the trip. My daughter was staying with my brother's girlfriend. This was the second night that she had stayed there. I got a call at 2 AM with Barb saying that my daughter could not breathe and to meet her at the emergency room. I left the youngest with my father and headed to the hospital. When the doors opened, my heart dropped. I could hear my daughter trying to breathe. What a horrible sound!

The doctors gave her a breathing treatment and she was on oxygen. The doctor asked all kinds of questions about vaccinations, asthma, etc. She was current on all vaccinations and this had not happened before. The hospital was small; the town only has a population of 3000 and the closest hospital was an hour's drive. After x-rays it was determined that her upper airway was swollen. The doctor called to consult with a pediatric specialist and, since she had strider and was not responding to treatment well, they wanted her to be transferred to the Children's Hospital. My response was, "Do it!" The catch was the EMTs at the current hospital were not qualified to give a tracheotomy, especially to a child if needed, and I could not fly with her. So the Life Flight helicopter was dispatched.

All I could think was, "Hasn't this child been through enough? Hasn't our family been through enough? My daughter was a huge "daddy's girl". My husband was unable to work due to his immigration status so he was the Mr. Mom of the family and primary care giver of the kids. It took months for her to adjust to the absence of her father. We went through nightmares, bed-wetting, becoming very sensitive to anything and the constant crying that she wanted her Daddy.

My daughter was airlifted to the Children's Hospital and my brother drove me. When we arrived, she was breathing normally but was attached to monitors. As a mother it is a very helpless feeling to see your child like that. The doctors said that her breathing stabilized on the flight and she had not had a reoccurrence. They monitored her every hour and dismissed her in the afternoon with a diagnosis of either croup or an allergic reaction to mold and mildew. It was a relief but, without exactly knowing what caused it, I am constantly worried.

I am going to retire for the night and attempt to get a few hours sleep before I have to arise at 5:30 AM.

My youngest awoke at 3:30 AM. His "overnight" diaper did not last overnight. What a marketing scam! After a diaper, PJ and bedding change, he would not settle down. So I put him in bed with me. I know all the "professionals" say that is not a good thing to do. I don't think they live my life and survive on the limited amount of sleep that I get so if it gets me and him uninterrupted sleep for the few hours I had left, I say, "Go for it!" I may pay for it later when he is older but I will deal with it then. Some nights I am tag teamed by the kids. When one is sleeping, the other is awake.

The morning routine went rather smoothly this morning. I arose at 5:45 AM after hitting the snooze a couple of times. I was able to get a shower, get ready, and get the dog out before the kids woke up. I pleased that everyone awoke with smiles on their faces today. No power struggle this morning. Maybe today will be smooth after all. I got the needed supplies for the youngest—diapers, blanket, change of clothes gathered the night before. I also made sure that my daughter had her alphabet item chosen for preschool. Today was 'W'. Although I was thinking something to reflect "Woman Power," she chose her wooden train whistle and proudly stated that it would cover two W's. Wooden and whistle. At times her knowledge amazes me. I feel guilty for not having extra time with her but she is as sharp as that "W" whistle.

At 7:10 AM we were driving to the first drop-off which is daycare for the youngest. He attends a wonderful home daycare. After pausing in the driveway for several minutes, babbling his piece with his finger pointed in the direction of the neighbor mowing the lawn, he was off towards the door. I know his language is total understandable to him and sometimes I can see the expression on his young face and know that he is thinking, "Mom, What is your problem? Don't you understand English?!" He waddled into the daycare, took his teacher's hand, threw up his right hand waved and said bye as he went to wash his hands. This is much better than the clingy, crying days that give me a guilt trip. I know that I don't have to worry about him while he is in the care of these people and that helps my sense of well-being. Today is a good day.

Back in the car for a 30-minute drive through massive

construction to drop off number two. My daughter is tired today so she snoozed in the back seat. That is quite a bit different than the usual. "Mom! Look at that! Mom! What is that! Why?" We arrive at preschool and gather up all her needed supplies including the wooden whistle and any other items of urgent needs such as the stickers for her friends and Ninja Turtle figure that goes everywhere with us. It is like another family member. We take her belongings to her cubby, and I sign her in. She says "Mom, Don't pick me up too early today. I want to play on the playground." Little does she understand I pick her up at the same time everyday and have little room to do otherwise. With hugs and kisses, I am off to work.

Once at work, I do the usual: check the e-mail and look at what is on my schedule for today. I work in a small satellite office on the East coast, south of the Mason-Dixon Line. Needless to say, it is a very male-dominated Southern environment. I find myself struggling with that on a daily basis. I do not consider myself an idiot; therefore, when I am spoken to as one,' it tends to enrage me. I surround my cubicle with pictures of my children to remind me of why I work. I currently have my Associates degree in accounting. I have worked in the Information Technology field for the last eight years or so. I am completing a Bachelor's degree in Information Technology. This is to give myself the confidence I need to do my job and pave the way for a promotion. I am paying for the education myself since my employer does not reimburse for the curriculum that I have chosen. With one paycheck, supporting a family and paying for my education has become a financial strain. I hope that one day I will win that lottery! As I sat in the weekly meeting we have, something that was said made me think back to another weekly meeting where it was stated by a peer that I do not like to work after 5:00 PM. I quickly explained that I had no choice. I do not have family here and my youngest child's daycare closes at 5:30 PM which is at least a 20 minute drive without traffic or construction. Besides, the late charge for daycare and the amount I would make for staying late would put me in the hole. It also reminded me of a time when I was seriously asked if I could get to work any earlier by a peer. My reply was "Hmmm..." If I don't sleep at all, it still won't matter because the earliest the daycare opens is 7:30 AM, and I am usually waiting in the driveway for them to open; so I guess that answer would be "No."

At lunch, I pondered my situation of my spouse. I am really frustrated with the government. I have learned more about the immigration process in this country than I cared to. The fact of the matter is we have followed the rules and are still waiting in BCIS (Bureau of Citizenship and Immigration Services) limbo. I hired a lawyer for the process that we needed to go through. The first step was to get a waiver of my husband's J1 Visa. The lawyer told us that only 40 percent of these type waivers were granted on the basis that we were filing under, which was extreme hardship. To make a long story short, the waiver was granted in February of this year. Five months later we are still waiting for the "processing" (or lack of) that will give my husband his K3 Visa to return home to his wife and children. As I mentioned, he left when our son was four-months old. We could not afford to keep my husband in school so he could legally stay here. When he left for his home country, which happens to share a border with Iraq, we knew that he would not be able to return just to visit. A visitor's visa won't be issued until his two-year residency requirement is met. Now we are waiting for the processing to take place for the visa that will allow him to return home. The frustrating part is I started the paperwork for this process in March, 2004. At that time the BCIS was currently working on paperwork received on January 10, 2004. Now it is the end of July and they are working on paperwork dated February 11, 2004. At this rate my husband will still be gone from us two years. BCIS is held to no deadlines. These people do not understand that the paperwork represents families' lives, children's lives.

One more frustrating aspect that I know of is a case where a U.S. citizen went to the country where my husband resides currently. This citizen arrived in the beginning of March, 2004 and married a woman from that country at the end of March. The foreign wife submitted and received paperwork from the U.S. Embassy in that foreign country and was allowed to return (she had been studying in the U.S.). How is that fair? She can come on a CR status because she has been married less than two years? But a man who has been married almost six years has to be put into limbo? His children have to suffer? His son may not even know who he is. When I wrote my Congressmen and Representatives, I was basically in so many words told, "Lucky for them; sucks for you." That really makes everything better. So we do the only thing we can: wait, hope, and pray that the process will speed up. My children have not seen their father in almost a year. In November it will be a year since I took them on that 11-hour plane ride.

I feel that the government has forced me to live as a single mother on one income. I was given a choice of taking my children to live with my husband in Turkey where we might not feel completely safe or to live as a single parent. What upsets me is marriage is so hard to begin with and the government wants to separate people like this. In some states, the separation duration I have experienced is enough to file for divorce under abandonment. But I don't see it as abandonment; I see it as a forced separation.

The rest of the afternoon was pretty uneventful. I rushed out the door at work promptly at 5:00 PM so I can pick up my daughter and still make it to my son's daycare by the 5:30 PM close time. It seems the only time that I really have alone is the time in the car to and from my daughter's preschool. That is a whole ten blocks a day! I picked up my daughter where she proudly announced that she lost her second upper front tooth. That is a total of four now. I asked where her tooth was and she disappointingly said, "Ms. Aletha lost it down the drain." It seems that her teacher was attempting to clean the tooth and it slipped from her hand and went down the drain. My daughter sympathetically said, "That is ok the Tooth Fairy saw it, and it is in the ocean." After all, that is where everything ends up when it goes down the drain right? I signed her out and off we went to pick up her brother.

After picking up both children, we headed home. On the car ride we had a discussion of what to have for dinner. The decision was fish sticks, mac 'n cheese, green beans and applesauce. Sounded good and easy to me! We arrived home and went through our routines. I took out the dog while the kids drank Kool Aid and ate a banana. I fixed the gourmet meal we had decided on and dinner went well without a hitch.

After dinner the kids watched some quality TV in Spongebob while I cleaned up, filled the dishwasher and started a load of laundry. Then it was bath time. After the bath we had just enough time for a snack and some Kim Possible before bed at 8:00 PM. That is my goal anyway. My daughter is my little party animal. She thinks that if anyone, including the dog, is up in the house, then she needs to be up too. Snack time brought a sibling argument. My son had just eaten the last yogurt and my daughter was not happy about it. The five-year-old genes kicked in. She informed me that she hated her brother and wanted to take him back to the hospital. She became angry and mean to me. I tried to tell her that I did not eat the last yogurt, and I understand her being angry with her brother but she did not need to be mean and nasty to me. "Oh, yes, I do," she said. I asked why? She proceeded to tell me, "Because you had him." After all was settled down, everyone went to bed fairly easily. I took some time to take inventory of what was needed at the store and begin my homework for the night before I got to go to bed and start all over the next day.

At the End of the Day

A child is a curly dimpled lunatic
~ Ralph Waldo Emerson

Sometimes I look back at my life and think, "How did I get here?" Before I had children, I had a well-paying job, traveled the world, wore designer clothes—the world was my oyster, so to speak. Now, I struggle to make ends meet, travel to and from schools, and wear sweats all day. However, my rewards now are far greater than anything I ever imagined. I can't imagine not having my children in my life. They are, by far, my greatest joy, my greatest accomplishment. I wouldn't want my life any other way.

~ Morgan C, 38, Oklahoma
"Happy where I am" mom of three (ages 17, 9, and 7)

After the laundry is folded and the kids are in bed, I feel like I should make time for my husband. But, as usual, my favorite TV show is on, and I just am not in the mood to "get down tonight." I know my husband is disappointed, but I think he's tired too. This weekend I'll try to spice things up with candles and lingerie, but tonight I'm going to be a TV slave.

~ Stephanie S, 42, Florida
TV-mom of four (ages 14, 10, 9, and 4)

So here I sit in bed, watching some mind-numbingly horrible television show, writing this diary and feeling the weight of guilt bearing down on me. I had no patience with the kids today, rarely checked in on my sick husband and just was not the person I strive to be. I feel like a bad mother, bad wife and a bad person. It's time for a reality check though. Life is made up of both good and bad stuff. Bad stuff is what makes the good stuff so good, right? So tonight I'll try to balance it all out with some good stuff—peeking in on my husband to make sure he's comfortably sleeping, watching my beautiful daughters peacefully sleep, and cuddling up with my son when he needs me in the middle of the night. I guess that's the stuff life is made of.

~ Joy G, 37, Colorado
Married mother of three (ages 6, 4, and 2 months)

We're getting ready to move to a new house in a few weeks. In the meantime, we are living with my in-laws. I know a lot of people complain about their in-laws—especially their mother-in-law, but I love mine. She is so helpful with the kids and really respects my authority as a parent. It's a little odd to say, but I'm going to miss living with them.

~ Becky C, 39, Colorado
Moving mom of two (ages 8 and 3)

After years of trying to attain my pre-baby size four, I have think I finally realize that I don't need to be thin to be loved by my family. Don't get me wrong. I want to look like those cute 20-year-olds, but they are just that—20-years-old. I just had my 40th birthday. I think I'll settle for looking like a cute 40-year-old instead.

~ LeAnn H, 40, New Jersey
Cute little mother of three (ages 20, 15, and 12)

While doing dishes tonight, I glanced at my husband watching the kids. He had this weird look on his face. I can't tell if it was contentment with our life, the desire to run away from it all, or total fear. I wanted to ask him, but I wasn't sure how he would react. Since our life is good and we're happy, I'm going to assume he is content.

~ Melissa W, 32, Canada
Assuming mom of three (ages 11, 9 and 6)

Now that I am a mom, I look at my mother and wonder how was she able to pull this parenting thing off without giving away the secret that you are flying by the seat of your pants! If this ever gets to print, then I want to say, "I LOVE YOU, MOM. THANK YOU!" The hardest thing about being a mom is learning that I will be the best mommy by being the best me first!

~ Jennifer B, 37, Southern California
Continually-in-training mom of two (ages 8 and 5)

I turn on the dishwasher, check on both boys and tell them one last time for the day that I love them, get ready for bed, and try to get into bed without waking Brian. He isn't fully asleep yet because, as I get into bed, he says, "I love you, honey. Thanks for working so hard today." I reply, "I love you too."

~ Cherie H, 34, Southern California
Loved mother of two (ages 2-1/2 and 7 months)

Thinking back on the days when my children were younger. I remember how my weary body bade to rest. I'd give my dog, Cocoa, her anti-epileptic pills and make sure she visited the backyard before bed. When I'd turn in, Cocoa would snuggle under my blankets, resting her head down by my toes at night. My big, king-sized bed seemed huge when my husband, Greg, was gone (he spent most of the week in San Jose where he worked). I especially missed him in those lonely moments before I drifted off to sleep.

~ Mary M., 51, Northern California
Then-weary mother of five (ages 28, 26, 24, 22, and 20)

Dear Diary,

...As I'm sitting here in the bath jotting down this diary. I realize how much of a girly-girl I am now that my daughter is here. I've always considered myself a "boy" mom. However, now I take more of an interest in my appearance, clothes, and the color pink. I also want to do girly-girl things with my friends like tea, shopping, and "chick" chat. This is a whole new world for me.

~ Tyler W, 30, Southern California
Reformed tomboy mom of two (ages 3 and 1)

We have been living in Guam for a year now. I really like it here. There is a sense of simplicity around us. I was born and raised in New York. I loved the excitement and craziness of it all. However, moving here has given me a sense of peace. I'm able to live in the moment, and I think my kids see that. My daughter commented today about how happy and relaxed I seem. I know that we will probably have to move back to the States soon enough, but I think I'd like to come back here to live permanently after my husband is discharged from the Navy.

~ Sonja J, 42, Guam
Content mother of two (ages 12 and 14)

10:00 PM: After an evening with my husband, I'm feeling much more centered in our relationship. It is so important to nurture it. I just checked on the kids and gave them one more kiss. Now, as I lie in bed, waiting for some late-night drama to run, I think about how grateful I am for my life. God has blessed me. I thank Him as I do each night for all my blessings. Joe gives me a kiss and is fast asleep. I know that sleep will elude me, but that's okay because I have my ongoing to-do list in my head along with 100 channels on TV to surf. <YAWN> Goodnight!

~ Juliet R, 37, Maine
Tired mother of three (ages 8, 4, and 3)

Dear Diary,
The kids are in bed, and I'm watching a reality show about swapping families. I wonder what kind of family I'd swap with. Would someone find out life completely weird? I think we are a typical family. We aren't perfect, but we do what we can to make it through the day.

~ Jodi M, 38, Missouri
Typical mom of two (ages 9 and 3)

Each day I like to write down everything I did. It makes me feel like I've accomplished something. So, do you know what I did today? I turned into my mom. I watched a video taken at my son's birthday party, and it hit me. I am my mom. I can't believe how much we are alike. I don't know whether to be thrilled or scared shitless!

~ Sheila C, 38, Rhode Island
Recycled mom of one (age 5)

I keep meaning to record what my husband, Joseph, said to me the other day, so I can always remember. He said, "You amaze me. Seeing you commit to giving birth naturally, and now breastfeeding, you're an amazing woman." He is so supportive and loving, but it also really lifts my spirits to have him recognize all my hard work, and my commitment to doing what I believe is best for our son. I never thought pregnancy and giving birth would be this much work, but it is truly the best thing I've ever done in my life, and I'm so thankful to share it with a man who is really with me. Going through this experience together has made us closer I'd ever imagined.

~ Rebecca V, 34, Southern California
Appreciated mother of one (age 2 weeks)

Finding a Connection

Marta, 45, West Virginia
Single mother of four

Marta, 45, is a single mother of four children (ages 30, 22, 12, 11), grandmother and writer. "...I am, first and foremost, a mother. A mother to four: two sons and two daughters. Each child radically different than the other. My experience with each just as unique. I am a writer. I'm an elder in the Presbyterian Church. That ministry is very important to me. I'm a collector of gargoyles. I am an avid accidental gardener. I throw seeds into the ground and clap my hands with delight and surprise when something comes up. I'm a foodie who loves to cook and, yes, I even like going to the grocery store. But, yeah...most of all, I'm a mother. It's a good life." Marta wants her children to go through life knowing her fierce love for them. She wants them to have the courage of their convictions. She also wants to play the bagpipes and win the lottery. "It can't buy love, but if you throw enough money at a problem, it usually goes away."

12:35 AM I lie awake, uncomfortable and stuffy. I know that it is not really that hot in my house; it's just that I like it very cold. I want to sleep snuggled under the covers even in the middle of summer. I would sacrifice heat in the winter to be cool in the summer. Hot is gross and sweaty. I can't sleep like this. The heat aggravates my lung disease. I fumble for my inhaler.

3:34 AM Well, that explains it. The AC wasn't even on. I had asked my youngest son, 12, to turn it on last night. It was the old "fake-off" again. He's getting very good at it.
"Did you brush your teeth?"
"Yes, Mom."
"Is that your homework?"
"Yes, Mom."
"Did you turn the AC back on?"
"Yes, Mom."
It's always, "Yes, Mom," and most of the time it's a lie. He tells me what I want to hear so I will shut the hell up and leave him alone. Some people tell me, "Oh, he's at that age." That's bullshit. There is no age at which lying is appropriate; I hate it that at this young age he is already tuning out females and not being a responsible member of the household. That's not the kind of man or husband I want him to be.

3:40 AM Ah, sweet relief. The icy air grips me and I climb back into bed and pull the comforter over my head.

6:00 AM Already? I get up to gain some coherence and balance. My oldest daughter has to be at work by 6:30 AM and

I'm not long after that. The dog and I go into the car and wait for her, silently observing the garden and the herbs and ornamental peppers we recently planted.

8:30 AM I call my son to try and rouse him so he will take care of the puppy he wanted. Neglect is a sure way to ruin a good dog. Why won't he get up? Why won't he take care of the things he says mean so much to him? I'm sure I had a hand in this somewhere; I just don't know how to right things. I'm not exactly certain what it is that I did that made him this way. He's not a bad boy. He's extremely intelligent and gifted. He's just not interested in anything outside of his own sphere or anything that requires him to move. But get him to talk about something he is passionate about and you'll fall in love with him.

10:00 AM I take a call on my cell phone about the house for rent in Pittsburgh. It's my oldest son's home. He's in prison. I have power of attorney. There's a mother's heartbreak for you. I was just fourteen years old when he was born. He was whisked away from me before we left the hospital. He went to live with his father's family because black families are tolerant and have the good sense not to let their babies be raised by someone else. It's not that my family didn't have good sense. My family worried about bringing up a black child in our seemingly white world. That's what they tell me now. I don't even remember what they told me then except that I should never feel guilty. Right.

I visit him occasionally and am always welcomed. But I never knew what my role should be in his life. And I didn't know how to play that role in his life and still live mine. That sounds so selfish now and maybe it was. I went to college. I fell in love with a man who would never understand. I had three more children. The list of things that man would never understand seemed to be never-ending. Or was it that he just did not understand me? Several years after we went our separate ways, I found my nerve and found my son—just before he went to prison. It was a good thing for both of us. The fact that I could be there for him now and help him with his affairs at this time has been good for both of us. It has leveled the playing field. I'm making up for lost time, and I think is has helped to erase any bitterness he may have had over my absence. But I cannot speak for him. He may feel nothing can explain away the absence of a mother and many years of questions. I love him. And I'm sorry. That is all I know to say. "I'm here now," sounds like such a stupid, petty excuse. But I am. I'm here now.

NOON I meet someone from the Worship Committee at the church for lunch. We have a lot to talk about and hopefully resolve. I have an "Aha! moment" when I realize this is the first time that I've ever gone outside to eat lunch. When did they get those nice picnic tables? It was beautiful. We plan to meet again for lunch.

2:00 PM I think summer is hard for kids. I call the house to check on the kids and make sure they're okay. We've done a couple of short weekend trips this summer, plan a couple more...we bought a decent pool, too. Still I think it is right about this time {July} that they start to look forward to school again.

4:00 PM I drive home to pick-up my son. My youngest daughter is staying with a friend. We run errands and grab a quick burger.

6:00 PM I work around the house and garden. I make two pounds of marinated mozzarella with fresh basil from my garden. I marinate meat to make jerky in the dehydrator. Now I am too tired to make dinner. That wasn't supposed to happen. I worry about not having my medicines anymore. The state took my transitional medical coverage away. My doctor has cancer and closed his practice. I make too much money on my job to get assistance with medicine. I'm a contract worker with the state and have no benefits. I have thyroid disease, hypertension, and COPD [lung disease]. I'm looking into herbal remedies. I can't die now. I'm having too much fun.

10:00 PM Hannah calls and wants to come home. I go and get her. My son pulls some lime margarita shrimp out of the freezer and makes them for us. Too spicy. I drink about a quart of soda to put out the fire in my throat. I play euchre on Pogo.com. I read the profiles of the other three players. All of them are women—mid-forties, same age range as myself. I like euchre because it isn't a dumb game; you have to think. But luck plays a part in it, too. I have to find a game site with more men. I don't mind hanging out with the girls. It would be nice just to talk to a man once in awhile.

The Search for the Perfect Nap

Sheryl C, 41, Missouri
Very tired mother of nine

Sheryl, 41, is a married mother of nine; only seven are at home right now (ages 13, 12, 7, 5, 3, and twins, age 2). Not one to miss out on any of the children's activities, she works from 10:00 PM to 3:00 AM Monday through Friday to be at home with her children in the day. Not one to worry about what others think, Sheryl's philosophy in life is to face it with a smile and a lot of laughter. Her children—all nine of them—come first in her life. "I am super proud of them. They are all well-behaved and caring and tons of fun to be with!"

12:00 AM I am in a trailer at the Earth City UPS hub. I have been her for one-and-a-half hours so far, and as I scan and load packages, my thoughts drift to my husband. He works 7 AM to 6 PM, I work 10 PM to 3 AM, and I try to sneak in a couple-hour nap before work. So, it is plain to see, we don't spend much time together. I need to work on some "us" time.

3:00 AM I just got off work and I am headed home to a hot shower and some sleep. Every muscle in my body is screaming. I am 41 years old and doing a job that I should have been doing when I was 19! When I get home, I tiptoe to each room and check on the kids. I listen at the top of the stairs—Kyle and Sam are quiet. They need to get up at 6 AM for school. My seven-year-old, Brian, is zonked in Maddie's, my three-year-old, bed with her. Blake, my almost six-year-old, is sound asleep on the floor in her room. The twins, Dane and Quinn, almost two —oh, they are so sweet, sound asleep with their little snoring going on. Oh, how I would love to wake them up to give them some squeezes! I restrain myself—after all, I am only looking at a good four-and-a-half hour sleep as it is.

8:30 AM Wake up "call" from seven-year-old, Brian, who bus comes at 8:41 AM. He insists that I get up and watch him get on the bus every morning. It makes him feel secure, I think. I would never let him down, even though, I would love to roll over and sleep a little longer. He has a field trip and needs a sack lunch. I jump up to make his lunch, only to find out that he has made it already. What a kid! I have no little drink boxes or cans of soda to send with him, so I tell him to get a drink from a water fountain while he's there. He looks so disappointed. I make a phone call to my trusty neighbor and, sure enough, she has a drink pouch to share. Whew! Got through another crisis!

I am sitting on our porch waiting for the bus to come; we are waiting and waiting. It is getting later and later and here comes the bus, but it's empty. The driver hollers out that there is no school due to a sewer pipe that broke. She informs me that it was announced on the news. Like, who would think to watch for school closings in May! Also, I put our TV in the garage 12 days ago—another story, another time. It is so nice without TV; more gets done and the kids are more imaginative with their time.

No more disappointments, no field trip, and Blake, my almost-six-year-old, was supposed to get his first chance to eat in the school lunchroom today as a practice for first grade. I call my retired mom and dad to see if they will take the kids to see "Shrek 2," which comes out today. They say they will and smiles, once again, are back on their faces.

9:20 AM Dane, Quinn and Maddie are still sleeping and

Brian and Blake are playing...maybe, I can squeeze in another half hour of sleep.

9:27 AM Dane and Quinn are being very verbal about getting out of their beds. Boy, that seven extra minutes of sleep was rejuvenating!

9:27-9:53 AM Got Dane and Quinn out of bed, changed their diapers and dressed them. All to them singing and laughing. What a joy it is to have them in my life! Threw in a load of laundry, after collecting various dirty clothes all over the house.

9:55-10:00 AM Made breakfast for five kids—three plates of waffles (the toaster kind, of course), one plate of pancakes (the microwavable ones, of course) and one bowl of cereal. They are all eating and having conversations...so cute! I grab a handful of cereal and a Hershey Kiss for my breakfast. An argument erupts about when Quinn and Dane's birth is—June 4 or July 4? I get called to settle it. It's June 4. Maybe, while they are eating, I can grab a few minutes of sleep.

10:05 AM I didn't even get horizontal. They thought that, since they were going to see Shrek, they should listen to the Shrek CD at an ear-splitting sound level. They are dancing and singing and having so much fun, that I think I will plop my fanny on the couch and enjoy them.

10:10 AM Well, that entertainment is over. Now, it is paper airplane soaring time. I have about eight to ten paper airplanes flying all over the room.

10:45–11:40 AM Mom, dad and my aunt come by to get Maddie, Blake and Brian for lunch and the movie, my aunt, in her 80's, is Quinn's best buddy. He just loves her! So sweet. My kids make me so proud when other people are around, they are so personable and I can tell that people enjoy them and the entertainment that they provide.

11:45 AM Well, it is just Dane, Quinn and myself. House is very quiet...messy, but quiet, except for the sounds of a "Barney" movie in the background. I need to make some phone calls to find out about football sign-ups for my 13-year-old, that, I believe, happened a while ago. I just haven't gotten around to taking care of it. I need to order a cake and get invitations out for Dane and Quinn's birthday party which is in just two weeks, and work on my 13-year-old's Bar Mitzvah which is only four months. I seem to work better under a little pressure to get anything done.

12:00–2:05 PM Okay, so I never made any phone calls! Instead, we went outside and Quinn and Dane played in water puddles and mud. They were having so much fun and were covered head to toe in water and mud. They kept saying, "Ewwww" and Yucky" over and over. Then we ventured over to my neighbor's house, where Dane proceeded to dump a tub of Playdoh on her carpet that she had just cleaned the night before. Luckily, she is like me, things like that don't really bother her. "Que Sera, Sera!" Dane and Quinn played with her one- and three-year-old and ate fruit snacks while I had a Diet Coke and a handful of pretzels and caught up on things with Janan, who offered to make Dane and Quinn's birthday invitations for me. It is so nice to have a friend who is crafty and is willing to help a busy Mom out. Brought Quinn and Dane home, cleaned them up, and put them down for a nap. Now, I will try for the phone calls that I need to make before my 12- and 13-year-olds get home from school, which is in 20 minutes.

2:20 PM I reflect on my day, so far. As much as I would love to get a nap in, I know it is not possible and I don't even know why I try every day. I have guilt feelings when I lie down or read a book, which I love to do, but seldom find a moment for it. I feel as if my time is wasted unless I am doing something productive in the house, be it laundry, dishes, playing with the kids, or straightening the house, which is an endless task. Time to myself seems selfish...I know, I know, we all need "our" times, and it makes us better moms to get some "us" time, but, I have never been good at relaxing. Oh, I try, just not very good at it; there always seems to be something else I could be doing.

2:30 PM Folding laundry and catching up with what my 13-year-old is into and up to. My 12-year-old stayed after school.

3:15 PM Sitting on the couch, reading what I have written in my diary so far. It seems that my days are not that exciting when it is put down in words. I enjoy my time with my children; they always tend to amaze me. They love nothing more than to play a board game or a card game with me. Ahhh, the simple pleasures of life. I beam with pride with each and every one of them. I could never imagine my world without them.

3:30 PM When I was thinking that I could grab a little

cat nap, in walk Maddie, Blake and Brian from their outing. They all start talking at once about their favorite scenes in the movie. My parents said that they were as good as gold. That's what I love to hear!

3:45–5:00 PM Wow! It finally happened. Maddie curled up on the couch with me and the next thing I know, it's 5:00 PM! Ahhh, the power of a nap! It took seven hours to finally get one, but it was well worth it. (Have you caught the major factor in my day yet? The search for a nap!) We woke up to Quinn's need for getting out of his crib from his nap.

5:00 PM Brian has a couple of friends over, and they are all playing baseball outside. I love hearing them play and argue and working things out amongst themselves. Time to think about dinner. (Which requires a prone position on the couch!)

6:15–7:15 PM Got through dinner—a "gourmet" feast of mac and cheese and apples. As I was cooking this elaborate meal, I realized that I was still in my pajamas! I have a hard time paying any attention to myself. I am sure my hair is sticking up; I never even glanced in a mirror at myself today. Got a few more loads of laundry folded and cleaned up the house.

7:30 PM Heading to grocery store, out of milk, juice, and diet soda. (Staples around here!) We go through nine gallons of milk a week around here, and my husband and I don't even touch it. Kids are giving me their list for treats to get while I am at the store—Krispy Kremes!

8:40 PM Krispy Kremes are a huge hit. They are all eating them and saying "Yummmmm" over and over again. I have an hour before I have to leave for work. I am debating whether to lie down for the hour or to hang out with the kids. Brian just informed me that I could lie down, that I have and hour or so before I have to leave. I think my kids understand my quest for sleep!

10:03 PM Well, I went for lying down, not sleeping, buy lying down, talking to the kids in the living room. Now, after putting the twins to bed, including changing diapers, getting all the necessary toys and books, I am going to be late for work. Hmmm, hugging my kids and getting kisses, or getting to work on time???? What a choice I have to make!

10:15 PM Made it to work just in the nick of time.

10:30 PM My full-time supervisor came up to me and asked how things were going, was I getting enough sleep, etc. I told him things were great. He said he just had an employee retention meeting, and he told everyone there that if he could bottle my enthusiasm and attitude, his job would be much easier. He didn't understand how I could always be so cheerful and have a smile on my face all the time. I asked him if he had kids. He said, "No." I told him that he wouldn't understand then.

12:00 AM Here I am scanning and loading packages in a trailer for UPS thinking about my husband and how I need to work harder on "US."

Proud To Be Me

Heide K, 45, Michigan
Single mother of three

Heide, 45, is the single mom of three (ages 18, 16, and 6). Not only a mom of a college student, high school student, and first grader, she is a published author, freelance writer, newspaper reporter/photographer and preschool art teacher. She's also a chauffeur, dishwasher, counselor, cleaning lady, ATM, Sunday School director, and owner of four cats. Facing life's obstacles, including two divorces and a child with ADHD, Heide handles adversity with perseverance and hard work. She prides herself in being the best role model for her children. "My children can look up to me. I am proud of myself!" For more about Heide, log onto www.thewriterslife.net/Kaminski.html.

6:30 AM Hit the buzzer for third time; I yell at my son, Tommy, to move over. As always, I wake-up right next to him. In his six years, he has not slept through a single night. At least now he just sleepwalks into my bed and doesn't wake me up anymore.

6:45 AM Drag myself out of bed, wash face, put on my usual anti wrinkle creams, plug in percolator, and check my email. Lots of junk mail.

7:00 AM My 16-year-old yells at me. She wants to be at school early, and I need to drive her. Tommy is not even up yet.

7:10 AM I'm dragging Tommy into van as he's still half-asleep. At least I had him dressed in his new clothes the night before, so there is one less thing to worry about in the morning.

7:25 AM Get 16-year-old to school. She rushes off, but remembers to holler "I love you, mommy." Too early to go to work, but too late to go back home. Decide to go to work anyway and drop Tommy off at the before/after school care.

7:30 AM Arrive at work and realize that I didn't give Tommy his Ritalin for his ADHD. Can't find my emergency pill bottle I usually carry with me. Have to turn around, because there is no way I can send Tommy to school without his meds.

7:45 AM Make it to work just in the nick of time. Time clock says 7:45 and 58 seconds. Whew!

8:00 AM Get called up front where the before/after school caregiver is getting the school kids ready to get on the bus. My son's giving his teacher grief while waiting in the bus line. His meds haven't kicked in yet. Can't afford to let him go onto the bus angry. Last time that happened he almost got kicked off the bus.

9:45 AM Disagreement with one of my two co-teachers. Try to smooth over it. Need job, need to get along with co-workers. I pray and beg God for a better job.

11:30 AM The kids have eaten lunch. One co-worker is on break, other one is trying to settle kids down for nap. I clean up the mess 20 little critters left on tables, floor and bathroom. No call from the school yet. Tommy must have made it through the bus ride and morning okay. Thank God! Last time I got a call from the school it was because Tommy spent one-and-a-half hours screaming in the principal's office, because he had to be escorted off the bus due to a little fight with another student. Noon My break! I am whipped. Turn on cell-phone. Text message from my best friend "Can't wait to see you at lunch!" Deane is what is commonly referred to as my "boyfriend". He's 53, so that term seems a little off. He is my best friend overall. Without his affection, attention, listening skills, and tons of other help, I would never be able to preserve my sanity while going through my divorce. We both live close to work and each other, so we take our break at the same time. We always meet at his house to share joys and griefs. He said he would marry me in an instant, IF I didn't have a small child. I don't blame him. He could be my son's grandpa.

12:45 PM On my way back to work when my ex-husband-to-be calls, "Can I borrow ten bucks?" For the umpteenth time I tell him "NO! You make way more money than I do; you haven't paid the mortgage, car payment and insurance for six months. What makes you think I have money, when you don't? What makes you think I would LEND you any if I had some???"

"Yeah, yeah," he says as he discounts my grief.

"Coming over tonight?" For the first six months after I left him, I told him I would work on "working things out" with him. But then he let the house WE own, but HE lives in go into foreclosure and the van WE own, but HE drove and trashed, get repossessed. Needless to say, that was the end of my rope.

3:45 PM Afternoon went OK. Tommy arrives back from school at the daycare where I work. No note or call from the teacher. Thank you, God!

4:45 PM My eight hours are up, but we have too many kids at the daycare still. Staff can't go home yet.

5:30 PM Finally, I can go home. 45 minutes overtime, but the ridiculous pay I get isn't worth the added stress. Tommy insists on having a friend over. His meds are wearing off, he's cranky. He raids the refrigerator and then complains "There is nothing good to eat." My 16-year-old calls "Mom, you have to pick me up at 6:15 PM."

8:00 PM Lunches for tomorrow packed, clothes for tomorrow laid out, percolator ready to be plugged in, dishes done, two loads of laundry done, a third in progress. Tommy is ready for bed. He watches cartoons, while I try to get some writing done.

8:45 PM Read story to Tommy, sent him to bed. My 16-year-old needs the computer for homework. I clean my office.

9:00 PM Deane calls and I decide to hop on over there for a little while to get some "me" time.

10:15 PM Back home. My 16-year-old is in bed, too, so I can use the computer for writing.

10:30 PM Ex calls "Sure you won't come over?" For the umpteenth time I tell him "NO!" He tries to tell me what I am missing. I know his game plan: he needs to find a new place to stay and doesn't want to pay rent. His car is crappy, and he is eyeing my van. He can't manage his money and pay his bills. No woman wants to get involved with him. So he's trying to schmooze his way back into my life. While I moved on and made something of myself, he went down the drain. I am not about to give up my accomplishments only to find myself back where I was two years ago with him.

11:30 PM I crash into bed. Wrote two stories for contests, worked some more on my children's book and finished editing a story for the newspaper. Almost two years ago I gave up being a stay-at-home mom, and I went to work for a daycare, so I could be near my son who has ADHD. I rented a duplex and got an old, but decent van. I keep up with all of my bills (barely), my home is decent, and we always have food to eat. I had two books published. Life as a single mom is very hard. But I have regained my dignity. And that makes me a better mom. My children can look up to me. I took the hard way out instead of staying in an ailing marriage. I am worn-out and tired, but at the end of the day, I am proud of myself!

Agent M.O.M.

Jenn E, 34, Southern California
Undercover mother of two

Jenn, married mother of two (ages 2 and 4), knows that to truly appreciate life and your children, you must accept the ups and the downs. "I think there is no better reward than being a mother—the love, laughs, tears and pain. Having a child who has suffered seizures, I've experienced all these emotions at different times and at once." Ever optimistic, Jenn's desire is to have a happy, healthy family that grows, laughs and appreciates one another. "I grew up with a very happy childhood and hope to pass that one to our kids."

Watch out, CIA Agent Sydney Bristow. Agent mom is on the go! I sometimes compare my hectic and crazy schedule as a stay at-home mom with a two-and-a-half and four-and-a-half year olds to that of the factious Special Agent Bristow on the television drama "Alias". However, she kicks ass and takes names only one night a week. I do it on a daily basis!

As I shuttle my daughter to preschool, speech class, playgroup, and ballet, I try to figure my plan of attack to fit in my son's nap, errands, work-outs, and other appointments. Like Sydney, I keep a tight schedule and stay focused both mentally and physically.

By bedtime, as the kids sleep peacefully, I tackle the home and husband. I always make sure I have some "me" time and "hubby" time. At the end of each day, I picture Sydney and say to myself, with a smile, "Mission complete."

Open All Night

Linda S, 38, Somewhere in the Distance
Pooped mother of three

When Linda Sharp, mother of three girls (ages 12, 10, and 7), popular columnist and author of ***Stretchmarks on my Sanity***, was asked to chronicle her life during a 24-hour period, she had her own thoughts. "...I mused over how many contributors would be able to literally snooze through the first six hours of the assignment. Entries would consist of a toss here, a turn there, followed by the letter Zzzzzz. Of course there would be those night owls for whom midnight spells laundry time, quiet time, infomercial time. I suspected there would be a fridge raid here or there, perhaps some sleep interrupted by the snores of the foghorn sharing their Sealy Posturpedic. And of course there would be a few new Moms whose nipples serve as an All Night Diner. Then there is me, neither power sleeper nor night owl. I believe laundry is best served at noon when I actually care enough to "Shout it out", and as for Home Shopping, I do not believe my life will suddenly be made better thanks to "four easy payments of $49.95". My hubby doesn't snore and my nipples have been returned to "recreational" status for many, many years now. I didn't think I would have much to offer a diary until my normal wake-up time of 4:30 AM, but then we got a puppy . . ."

MIDNIGHT: Things That Go Poop in the Night

Just as sleep reducing as is the piercing cry of a new born, so is the plaintive whine of a puppy. I attempt to ignore the sounds coming from her crate on the floor next to my bed . . . whine, whine, scratch, wiggle, whimper. With uncanny precision, each time I begin to fall back into REM, I am yanked back into DAMN. Dear God in heaven, whose idea was this scrap of fur?!?!?

Staring at the red numbers of the clock, 12:07 AM, I know all too well the answer. Me. After successfully dodging the I-want-a-pet bullet for eleven years, I was shot through the heart by a one pound four ounce sniper with a wet nose. Actually it is more accurate to say I was shot through the head, for nothing else can explain the gear that suddenly slipped in my cerebrum and allowed the word "Yes" to be emitted, making me the proud owner of "the noise".

All too aware that ignoring the cry will result in a repeat of the previous night's 2 AM feces frolic and subsequent bath, I roll out of bed for the second time since 9 PM, remove her from her crate and head out the back door to sit in the porch light's harsh glare, chanting, "Go poopy. Go poopy. Go poopy." I stare into the darkness of the backyard and wonder if Gandhi ever did that with new monks?

2:16 AM - OH-MY-GOD

Does she even have a bladder?!?! Out we go again. Her to the grass, me to my mantra. Glancing up to the heavens, I wish on a star that my out-of-town husband is stricken with nocturnal diarrhea, a lumpy mattress, and a couple who specialize in loud fornication and headboard reggae in the next room.

4:30 AM - Who Let the Dogs Out? Me, me, me, me, me.

What $#@! irony. As I slam the alarm off button on the Baha-ha Men, the furry dictator decides it is once again time to pee. Doesn't she know I get up at the butt-crack of dawn so I have time to myself??? I assume the position in my lawnchair and she proceeds to . . . stare at me. I swear, if she does not assume her position in two seconds, I am going to squeeze her until some form of juice comes out!
Lucky for her, she squats.

Then this creature, who could easily have her ass kicked by a guinea pig, walks over to me, looks up and tilts her head. I melt.

4:44 AM - Checking My Look in the Mirror

With Cruella de Dog back in her crate, I seek refuge in my bath-room. And I do mean refuge. I love my bathroom. It is equal in size to my master bedroom, larger actually because of the two walk-in closets. I, of course, have the larger one, complete with a separate walk-in area for my shoes. No, you won't find

Manolo Blahniks ala Carrie Bradshaw in "Sex & the City," but you will find everything from evening-wear satins to soccer Mom sneakers, all of which look great and none of which I paid more than $50 each. Take that, Sarah Jessica Parker.

My bathroom has separate counters and sinks to divide my beauty products (creams, lotions, exfoliants, gels, make-up, bronzers, shampoos, conditioners, utensils, candles) from his (soap). My tub has a window; there are high ceilings and flattering light, although at 4:44 AM, every bulb may as well be fluorescent. I look like crap, and for the millionth time in my life, know that if I did not know how to use all those products to transform the hag staring back at me, I would impale myself on an eyelash curler.

5:30 AM - Walk Softly & Carry a Big Cup of Tea

I tiptoe out of my bathroom and bedroom so as not to disturb Her Highness in the crate. Dammit! The door squeaks as I close it and I hold my breath waiting to see if she notices. Silence. Sheesh, this is just like having a baby all over again. The kids are still in bed, so I make my tea in peace, savoring the stillness, enjoying the quiet. This is my time and I am severely protective of it. Let the rest of the world slumber, I prefer to read, work, answer e-mail, scan CNN, pee alone. This morning I choose to read a few chapters of a new bestseller while enjoying my tea. I tuck into the corner of the couch, open the book and . . . fall back asleep. The next thing I know, the sun is up, my ten-year-old is poking me in the arm demanding breakfast and informing me that the dog peed in her crate.

7:49 AM - Oh yes, They Call Her the Streak

As the ten-year-old and the newly bathed puppy enjoy breakfast, I enjoy washing the bedding. Coming out of the laundry room, I am met by a still sleepy, buck-naked seven-year-old, trailing a blankey. I swear, this child missed her true generation by forty years. She is a clothing optional flower child trapped in a clothing mandatory millennium. She would rather be nude than attired, regardless of the weather or temperature. I guess if I were shaped like a stick of gum I may view things differently, but, as it is, I believe cellulite is meant to be pantsed, not paraded.

She begins to head to the kitchen table and I stop her. Call me crazy, but I enforce the rule followed by all professional nudists: There must be something between your cheeks and your chair. It's just good nude etiquette. Grumpily she heads back up to her room to grudgingly apply a pair of underwear. Now I can serve her a Pop Tart.

All restaurants have standards, I think to myself, as I turn and slip in a fresh puddle of dog pee.

9:53 AM - Spam for Breakfast, Anyone?

While my younger two daughters play with their puppy, I head to the computer. Signing on, I hear the familiar "You've Got Mail". And how! 659 this morning. That is, unfortunately, average for me. Yes, many are worthy of opening and need a response—editors, assignments, questions, admirers, but the rest? A pile of SPAM big enough to feed Cleveland.

Owning a website is a great thing, I enjoy it. Sanity Central, started as a way to simply make parents laugh, has grown to become one of the most popular parenting sites online. Authors, columnists, cartoonists, contests, fun, all can be found there. However, who are also in residence are the "characters" that made up the original site. Cartoon "experts" on everything from fitness to sex to parenting are a popular staple of the site and all of them have their own email addresses. As the warped brain behind all their personalities and replies, all their email forwards to my main inbox for attention.

Ergo, I get not one offer to make my penis larger!, buy drugs in Canada!, reduce my debt!, refinance my mortgage!, become a minister (did that already!)!, view free porn!!, lose weight!, gain confidence!, make money!, look younger!, but ten.

Yes, power SPAM. And yes, I have filters, but anyone online knows that the spam marketers stay one slimy step ahead. The latest filter—avoiding tactic? Throw a period in or misspell the main word. Is Y.ur Panis Small? Personally, my panis would have to be almost nonexistent before I resort to buying a drug from someone with hillbilly grammar.

After five solid minutes of banging the delete button, I turn my attention to the emails that made the cut only to discover a reminder that today is the day I am supposed to record two Lighten Up With Linda Sharp segments for a radio show. Damn!

10:16 AM - Wake Up, Sleeping Beauty

"Mom, the dog peed on the carpet!" I abandon my panic over what to record long enough to clean the carpet and begin to wake my eldest daughter, a 12-year-old whose power sleeping qualifies her for the Teenager Olympics. She will resist daylight to the final Z, clinging to her pillow much like Rose clung to her scrap of wreckage as both Jack and the Titanic went down around her.

I pull, I poke, I invoke the "Mom Voice" and use her middle name. Nothing. Fine. I drop the puppy on her head and hope she pees.

The puppy does the trick as that little tongue disappears up my daughter's nose, happily finding a mid-morning snack of boogers. My daughter sits up, and I shake my head. How? How can someone wake up after such a hard sleep and look ready for a Cosmo cover shoot? When is it that we stop looking ravishing in the morning and begin to simply look ravaged?

NOON - Who Moved My Cheese?
I have finally narrowed it down to the two pieces I am going to record in two hours; however, now I must narrow those down, as each humor segment can only be one minute 45 seconds. As I begin to condense my humor, hunger pangs remind me the sun must be high overhead. This can wait, my stomach cannot.

Heading to the kitchen, I spy my daughters working covertly at removing a new spot of urine from the carpet. All three faces turn towards the noise of my approach and freeze in a rictus worn only by dead people and those caught working covertly to remove a new spot of urine from the carpet.

I take over, reminding them that the $#@$ dog needs to be taken out more often than once a day and that if they ignore her to this point again, I shall clean the carpet with the shirts they

are wearing, while they are wearing them.
I resume my trek to the kitchen, intent on enjoying my daily favorite snack of fresh hunks of Parmesan Reggiano, fresh off the wheel at the gourmet food store. Cut me some slack, my shoes are cheap, remember? I am allowed to indulge in something small. Opening the vault (meat drawer) where it is safely ensconced, it is immediately conspicuous by its absence.

"Who moved my cheese?!?!?"

My youngest daughter walks in and informs me that Daddy took the rest yesterday afternoon to eat on the plane, but that there are lots of those orange square cheeses left. Clouds form over my head. I now add to my wishlist that his hotel runs out of water while he is showering, at the same moment the fire alarm goes off and he has to evacuate to the street clad only in bubbles and a hand towel. Oh, I also hope he gets bound up from eating that much cheese—it was a large hunk.

1:50 PM - Quiet on the Set
With edited copy in hand, I give the usual instructions to my daughters before heading to my "studio" to wait for the radio host to call and record. "Stay away from the front door. Be quiet. Keep an eye on the dog. Be quiet. Keep the TV turned down. Be quiet. And if you value your life, BE QUIET."

I enter my "studio", the area you already met, my shoe closet, and breathe deeply. Not because I enjoy the mingled smell of leather and foot odor, but because no matter how many times you do one of these things, you still get a little nervous that you'll screw up too many times and not have your contract renewed.

The phone rings, we make small talk for a few minutes, and then begin the process. Thankfully, today all the mishaps and redos stem from goofs and gaffes on her end. I am safe for another two weeks.

2:17 PM - UFO - Unidentified Falling Object
Emerging from the studio, ok, ok the "shoedio," I walk right into the dog taking a power poop on my bedroom floor. My daughters are nowhere to be seen.

I holler "No!" and grab the dog in mid-poo, literally it is still half in/half out, and run her to the back door, of course jiggling off the outer portion along the way. I plop her in the grass and she resumes activity. This is good, because the best way to housebreak pets is to catch them in the act and correct it immediately. I feel good until I walk back in to clean up the "fallen comrade" and find a pile in the corner of the room.

My daughters sheepishly apologize and then proceed to accuse each other of "supposed to have been watching her!" This from the same children who swore on their eyes they would love, honor, protect and play with this dog till college do us part. As if I actually had any illusions about whose dog this would be—why do you think I waited 11 years?

To irk them and make them rethink their errant ways with the pooch, I walk away singing the song I composed at 2:30 AM while trying to get back to sleep:

When you wish upon a star
That your dog's struck by a car

When you wish upon a star
Your dreams come true.

Like a bolt out of the blue
I will strike you with my shoe
Pee again upon my rug
I'll flatten youuuuuuuu...

2:30 PM - Let's Get Physical
With the dog in her crate for a nap and the children in their crates (rooms) for an afternoon reading session, I don a jog bra, shorts and running shoes and head back to my office which, by virtue of the treadmill, bun/thigh machine and free weights, doubles as my workout facility. Like my morning tea time, exercise time is mine and mandatory. Gravity and I are locked in a battle over the placement of my buttcheeks, and I am not going down without a fight.

Actually, at 38, I am holding it together rather well. At f5'2", I weigh in at 98 pounds, and have good tone and definition. To anyone who vomits at that sentence, don't. It did not happen by magic and I am naturally short, not naturally thin. I have to constantly police what I eat, trading Twinkies for a taut tummy (well, as taut as a tummy can be after three births and no plastic surgery). I also freely admit to a healthy amount of vanity that is the impetus for facing the treadmill at least five times a week.

I shut the door, crank the music—current faves to sweat to? Bon Jovi, Weird Al and Clay Aiken. Shut up. My ass is smaller than yours, so nyah.

3:38 PM - Mail Call!
Sweaty and triumphant, I head to the mailbox humming a classic Weird Al parody of the Back street Boys "I Want It That Way," called "I Bought It On eBay." Opening the box, I am happy to see a package I bought on eBay inside. Being the cheapest person alive, I constantly haunt that site for everything. Did you know that, in addition to finding antique outhouse corncobs, you can also bid on brand new, in their packaging items such as make-up, perfume, and video games? Today's package contains Strivectin SD, yes, the stretchmark cream everyone raves about, but is exorbitantly priced at $135, if you can find it in a store. I have lucked into a brand new tube for half that price, plus minimal shipping.

(And yes, for your information, the product does appear to work. After one month, my stretchmarks are noticeably lighter and my crow's feet are now more like crow's toes.)

4:00 PM - The Game of Life
Released from the bonds of forced literary enjoyment, my daughters convene downstairs for a promised game of Life with Mom. While they all choose to eschew higher education, I go the college route, amassing $100,000 in debt before my first spin of the wheel. Actually make that $110,000, as I have to pay my daughter, whose career card reads "Computer Technician," $10,000 as a fee to fix the wheel I spun wrong and is now stuck between numbers.

Moving forward, I finally am able to choose both Career and Salary cards. Great. Even with my higher education, I end up being an Artist with a $20,000 payday. My only hope now is to land on a "Trade Salary Card with Any Player" space and zing the daughter who is a Sports Star with the coveted $100K card.

We move on through the game, they gleefully pulling in large wads of cash each Payday, landing on bonus spaces such as "Win Nobel Prize, Collect $150,000". Me, I am unable to buy a house, I live in my car, am in debt up to my eyelashes and inevitably land on spaces like "Host an Online Concert. Pay $100,000". Oh, and I manage to artfully dodge those pesky "Trade Salary Card" spaces.

The game ends with me living in a forest, paying off my student loan debt by selling my own plasma. Lesson for my daughters? Don't go to college. Unless Parker Brothers are paying for it, that is.

5:12 PM - My Husband, the Idiot

Daddy calls from his hotel before heading out to dinner with fellow executives. They are going to a restaurant I have seen profiled on both The Travel Channel and in Wine Spectator. I am not; therefore, add to my wishlist one case of food poisoning and severe anal leakage that will strike just as his morning meeting gets underway.

When will hubbies learn that they should never truly discuss the details of their dining when they call? Especially when they have stolen the last good cheese at home? Moms routinely make meals out of breadcrusts and by licking the inside of the baby food jars. Tell us you are going out to a planned dinner—that is fine—we understand. But under no circumstances sound excited, brag or embellish the dining destination. In fact, flat out lie. "Yes, honey, there is a planned conference dinner tonight, they have managed to reserve a wing at the Shoney's just off the interstate. They promised it is near the salad bar."

Hanging up the phone, I look down. The dog just peed on my shoe.

5:30 PM - Haute Couture in a Kmart World

With my yellow tennis shoes in the washing machine and a new white pair on my feet (Payless, Buy 1 Pair, Get The 2nd Half Price), I announce that we too are going out to eat. Pandemonium ensues at the thought of glasses with straws and adults to kiss their butts standing at the ready.

The girls run off to change and return in fresh shorts and tops; well, two of them do. The middle daughter appears dressed for a night at the opera (Christmas dress, hose, patent leather shoes), not the local Chinese buffet. She is a diva from the word go. I think that she emerged wearing a feather boa and tiara, but the nurses had to remove them to weigh her.

Sent back upstairs to dress down like the rest of us, she punctuates her displeasure by stomping each step, stopping just short of slamming her door—she knows better. A slammed door in these parts insures immediate punishment, like scooping the backyard.

She comes back down, still clinging to her Divadom by way of a slathering of lip gloss and sunglasses, ala Paris Hilton, defiantly on her face—it is night and raining.

I give up. "Get in the car."

6:00 PM - I'll Have the Special, Please

We enter our favorite Chinese restaurant, unassuming in its strip mall location, but outstanding in its stellar buffet, and are recognized by the staff—we eat here often.

Shown to our table, the girls place their drink orders and head off to the bounty that awaits. I admit, I love this place for the food, even more so for the fact that every person in my family can find something to be happy about here. It is always a pleasant dining experience and the girls are able to escape the usual Kids' Menu of Chicken Fingers, Hot Dog or Hamburger. Plus they get to make their own desserts, a surefire crowd pleaser. But the main reason I love this place is the fact the cooks and bussers stare at me while I choose my sesame chicken, hot & sour soup and egg roll.

Get over it. I'm a mother of three children. I'll take any form of flattery I can get at this point in my life!

7:07 PM - What's in a Name

With both my appetite and my ego sated, we head back to the minivan. I am stuffed, as are the girls. All we want are elastic pants and bed. As we tool down the road, we crank Radio Disney and sing along with Lindsay Lohan, Hilary Duff and Raven. Do they even play anything else? Oh yeah, they play Hoobastank too. Hoobastank. Hoobastank. Hoobastank. Hoooooooobastank. Sorry, I love saying that word. Plus you know they came up with that band name one night while they were drunk, farting and talking like Mushmouth from Fat

Albert. "Fffffffffttttttttppppppp." "Eeeeeeewwwba, dudeba! Hoobastankba itba up inba hereba?"

I need some sleep.

7:29 PM - Release the Hounds!
We enter the house to hear incessant whining and scratching. I race to the crate and grab the dog, heading in full gallop mode to the back door. We make it just in time. Good girl! (The dog too.)

7:43 PM - A Walk in the Park
Much to everyone's chagrin, I insist we take the dog for a walk before bedtime. This is not some canine philanthropy on my part. I just know she will be tired and have an empty colon after a good walk. Both of which play into my grand scheme to actually sleep more this night.

We set out, leash in one hand, snack-sized Zip Lok in the other (this is a one pound dog, remember?). Like clockwork, less than two minutes into the trek, my plan is working! She is squeezing out her "final thought" for the evening. I turn the baggie inside out and retrieve her offering, zipping it up immediately. I like that I'm a responsible dog owner. My daughters just like the way it steams up the baggie.

As we trot along, fellow dog walkers laugh at the site of our hound. From across the street, she looks like a dust bunny on a leash. We walk on, head and steaming bag of poo, held high.

8:08 PM - Good Night, Irene

With the kids tucked in and the dog's tanks on empty, I place her in the crate, cover it with towels and turn on my sound machine. I figure if it helps me sleep, why can't it work on a dog?

I head back into my bathroom sanctuary, and set to removing the contacts from my eyes, the day from my face, the sesame seeds from my teeth. I climb into my softest shorts and T-shirt and crawl out to enjoy my bed. I hit the remote and fall asleep watching a Cosby Show rerun—the one where Bill Cosby dreams he gives birth to an enormous sub sandwich.

8:57 PM - Signing Off
I roll over and in my half-sleep and manage to hit the off button on the remote. My wonderful high tech TV makes its highly irritating "Bloopbloopbloopbloop" on / off sound. No. NO. NOOOOOO!

The whining starts as the dog decides she needs to bloopbloop too.

9:01 PM - Go to Sleep, Take Two
Back in her cage, back in my bed. Zzzzzzzzzzzzz

11:17 PM - There is a Devil; She is Black & Furry
I am stolen from a wonderful dream involving me, George Clooney and a sub sandwich by the whining of the crate spawn. We head to the backyard and she has the good sense to quickly squat and walk back to me. I give her a liver treat in thanks and we both go back to bed.

MIDNIGHT - You're Still Here?

Zzzzzzzzzzzzzzzzzzzzzzzzzzzzzzzzzzzzzzzzzzzzzzzzzzzzzzzzzzzz
zzzzzz

List of Participants

"Some people come into our lives and leave footprints on our hearts..."
~ Flavia Weedn, Forever

Allard, Shawna	San Marcos, CA
Altan, Lisa	Winston-Salem, NC
Allen, Susan	Portland, OR
Amsterdam, Michelle	Land O'Lakes, FL
Anderson, Maria	Cerritos, CA
Anonymous	Southern CA
Baccanari, Melinda	Chula Vista, CA
Bartee, Susanna Hickman	Germany
Baumer, Mary Elizabeth	Wausheka, WI
Benefield, Jennifer	San Marcos, CA
Bennett, Sara P.	Sacramento, CA
Brokus, Sami	Abingdon, MD
Cambridge, Morgan	Edmund, OK
Campbell, Becky	Longmont, CO
Clark, Jennifer	Chicago, IL
Coates, Sheila	Providence, RI
Combs, Leslie	Canada
Coulter, Sheryl C	St. Louis, MO
Cousineau, Kelley Cunningham	Maplewood, NJ
Davis, Felicity	Reno, NV

Dillow, Elizabeth A	Colo Springs, CO
Dix, Linda	Ballwin, MO
Doe, Rachel	San Diego, CO
Davies, Ann	Richmond, VA
Druxman, Lisa	San Marcos, CA
Elovitz, Jenn	Encinitas, CA
Eschner, Kelly	Milwaukee, WI
Evans, Jennifer	Raleigh, NC
Fernandes, Carey J	San Marcos, CA
Frank, Crystal	St. Paul, MN
Gallagher, Kathy	San Marcos, CA
Gianulis, Samantha S.	San Diego, CA
Gibbons, Joy	Denver, CO
Glancy, Amy	Encinitas, CA
Gorman, Cathy	Twin Falls, ID
Hamilton, LeAnn	Aberdeen, NJ
Harris, Natalie	Oakland, CA
Hedberg, Kathleen Coates	La Mesa, CA
Heid, Cherie	San Marcos, CA
Howard, Trish	Santa Ana, CA
Jabbari, Kimberly Lynn	Carlsbad, CA
Jackson, Holly	Austin, TX
Johnson, Sonja	Guam
Johnson, Angie	Bakersfield, CA
Jones, Laurie	Greeley, CO
Kaminski, Heide AW	Tecumseh, MI
Kennedy, Michele	Tempe, AZ
Korrs, Tina	Pittsburgh, PA
Lawrence, Deidre	Ann Arbor, MI
Mallory, Darcy	Kansas City, KS
Mathews, Jodie	St. Louis, MO
Martin, Marta	Charleston, WV
Metz-English, Carrie	Hurley, SD

Miller, Lisa	Cincinnati, OH
Moland, Tracy Lyn	Canada
Morrill, Mary Borley	San Jose, CA
Morris, Jennifer	Grand Junction, CO
Mumm, Deborah	Grayslake, IL
Murphy, Tish	Santa Ana, CA
Nallis, Monica	Akron, OH
Nelson, Nicole	Albuquerque, NM
Nolan, Stacie	Houston, TX
Olsen, Claudia	Cedar Rapids, IA
O'Reilly, Margaret	Jacksonville, FL
Osternik, Sara	Encinitas, CA
Paulson, Christin	Los Angeles, CA
Paterson, Tara	Round Hill, VA
Patterson, Suzanne	Montgomery, AL
Powell, Sarah	Syracuse, NY
Potter, Ellen	Buffalo, NY
Robbins, Juliet	Portland, ME
Richards, Vickie	Waterbury, CT
Rose, Joy	Hastings, NY
Robinson, Andrea	Englewood, CO
Sanchez, Tina	Las Vegas, NV
Schmitt, Paula J	Chelsea, VT
Scott, Heather	Indianapolis, IN
Sharp, Linda	Somewhere, USA
Sieler, Tonya	Vancouver, WA
Smith, Julie	San Marcos, CA
Smith, Stephanie	Middleburg, FL
Smith, Tiffany	Carlsbad, CA
Suman, Michelle	Bellefontaine, OH
Sutter, Stacy	Cass County, ND
Stratford, Mary	Cody, WY
Taylor, Donna	San Rafael, CA

Thomas, Jessica	Marlton, NJ
Turner, Rebecca	Billings, MT
Van Ness Lacko, Rebecca	Corona, CA
Vega, Jeannie	Norway
Wagner, Tyler	Ventura, CA
Walker, Melissa	Canada
Weller, Margorie	France
Ward, Leah	Rochester, NY
Wright, Emily	Portland, OR
Wells, Helen	Ft. Myers, FL
Williams, Terry	Denver, CO
Yeats, Toni	Santa Rosa, CA
Young, Sara	Modesto, CA

Giving Back

A bit of fragrance always clings to the hand that gives roses.
~ Chinese Proverb

The greatest strength of a community is the potential for everyone to take action and get involved! **Mommyhood Diaries: Living the Chaos One Day at a Time** supports this commitment to creating meaningful community relationships by assisting homeless moms and their families. A portion of the book sales will be donated to Dress for Success and St. Vincent de Paul's Village in San Diego, California.

Fostering a Mama-to-Mama Community

A friend is one of the nicest things you can have,
and one of the best things you can be.
~Douglas Pagels

Mommyhood can leave you feeling isolated and, sadly, inadequate if you feel disconnected. Satisfy the powerful urge to connect with parents by fostering a mama-to-mama community by joining a moms' group. Moms' groups allow you to reach out to others who relate to your feelings of awe, frustration, and exhaustion. Moms can also provide you with stimulating conversation that is lost on your child. Check with your doctor for a local group. If you can't find one, start your own group like Mommy Mentors.

Mommy Mentors is a monthly discussion group that provides an opportunity to bond with other mamas who, just like you, are muddling through the chaotic, endearing, and always unpredictable world of parenthood. So make it a mom's night (or day) out and join us for a chance of lifelong mama-to-mama connections and idea exchanges.

Starting a Mommy Mentors chapter in your neighborhood is as easy making Kraft EasyMa. Receiving this additional maternal support is essential during the early stages to feel linked in your new role as mommy. For more information on fostering a mama-to-mama community, log onto www.mommyhullabaloo.com.

About the Author

Fill your paper with the breathings of your heart.
~ William Wordsworth

Proud wife, mother of three, entrepreneur, writer, and reigning chaos queen, Julie Watson Smith relinquished the dream of perfection and now lives comfortably in the chaos of mommyhood, one day at a time.

Julie is the founder of AgeLink Intergenerational Programs and owner of Mommy Hullabaloo, a life management company that inspires moms to learn, live, and love the chaos of mommyhood. Additionally, Julie pens a humorous parenting column of the same name. "Mommy Hullabaloo" has been heralded as the perfect blend of heart and humor. Find out more about Julie at www.mommyhullabaloo.com!

We empower mom writers.

Publishing the Works of Extraordinary Mom Writers

Wyatt-MacKenzie Publishing, Inc

WyMacPublishing.com